Macramé

Beginners

Learn And Master Skills of Macramé With A Complete Step-By-Step Guide.

By

DAISY ARNOLD

© **Copyright 2022 by DAISY ARNOLD- All rights reserved**.

This document is geared towards providing exact and reliable information regarding the topic and issue covered.

- From a Declaration of Principles which was accepted and approved equally by a Committee of the American Bar Association and a Committee of Publishers and Associations.

In no way is it legal to reproduce, duplicate, or transmit any part of this document in either electronic means or printed format. All rights reserved.

The information provided herein is stated to be truthful and consistent, in that any liability, in terms of inattention or otherwise, by any usage or abuse of any policies, processes, or directions contained within is the solitary and utter responsibility of the recipient reader. Under no circumstances will any legal responsibility or blame be held against the publisher for any reparation, damages, or monetary loss due to the information herein, either directly or indirectly.

Respective authors own all copyrights not held by the publisher.

The information herein is solely offered for informational purposes and is universal, and the presentation of the information is without a contract or any guaranteed assurance.

The trademarks that are used are without any consent, and the publication of the trademark is without permission or backing by the trademark owner. All trademarks and brands within this book are for clarifying purposes only and are owned by themselves, not affiliated with this document.

Contents

Introduction	7
Chapter 1: The Beginnings of Macrame	10
1.1: Where Macrame Got Its Start	11
1.2: Macrame without the Use of Tools	14
1.3: The Beginning of Contemporary Macrame	17
1.4: Some Advantages of Using Macrame	19
Chapter 2: Macrame Terminologies	23
Chapter 3: Tools and Materials	28
3.1: Project Board	29
3.2: T-Pins	31
3.3: Patterns	32
3.4: Scissors	34
3.5: Precision Tweezers	36
3.6: Rotary Cutter	37
3.7: Crochet Hooks	39
3.8: Corkboard	40
3.9: Macrame Rope	42
3.10: Cotton String	43
3.11: Embroidery Floss	44
Chapter 4: Principal and Useful Knots	45
4.1: Lark's Head Knot	46
4.2: The Cow Knot	47
4.3: A Knot Tied in Half	48
4.4: Square Knot	49

4.5: The Knot Overhead	50
4.6: The Spiral Stitch	50
4.7: The Clove Hitch	52
4.8: Chinese Knot	53
Chapter 5: Choosing Materials for Macrame	55
5.1: Tweezers for fine detail work & crochet hooks	59
5.2: Needles	60
5.3: Comb of Fringes	60
5.4: Macramé Bead Smith Board (Macramé Bead Board)	61
5.5: Tape	62
5.6: Shook	63
Chapter 6: Macrame Projects	67
6.1: Summer Macrame Bag	67
6.2: Macrame Cactus Toy	73
6.3 Macrame Bracelet	77
6.4: Macrame Coasters	80
6.5: Macrame Pencil Case	83
6.6: Home Décor	87
6.7: Hammock	91
6.8: Macramé Leaves and Feathers	94
6.9: Wallcoulding Macrame	98
6.10: Macrame Flower	106
6.11: Macrame Boho Tassel	109
6.12: Macrame Garlands	112
Chapter 7: How To Avoid Principal Error?	115

7.1: Study Basic Knot	118
7.2: Start With Hemp Cord	119
7.3: Use Right Materials and Equipment	122
7.4: Start With a Simple Project	124
7.5: Keep The Ends from Fraying	125
7.6: Make Uniform Knotting	128
7.7: Be Patient	129
Conclusion	131

Introduction

Macramé is a centuries-old technique used to manufacture decorations and fabrics with many knots. This strategy may rapidly and cheaply personalize and decorate your home. Because there are many ways to mix knots, you can build beautiful and useful things. Macramé is usually hung from the ceiling or tied to a macramé board. It's a knotted cloth popular in the Philippines. When knotted together, they generate full- and double-half-hitches.

Macramé is a flexible fiber craft that may be used to make wall art, plant hangers, jewelry, purses, and clothing. Macramé may be modest or elaborate, fashioned with cotton thread, jute, flax, or yarn. Adding decorations like beads and threads may broaden design choices. Given their knot-tying talents, it's hardly a surprise that sailors spread macramé everywhere. They used it to pass the time at sea and then negotiated or sold it once they arrived, transporting it to China and North America. British and American seafarers invented hammocks, belts, and bell fringes in the 1800s.

Macramé gained popularity in the 1970s after a slump. It made wall hangings, plant hangers, decorations, and even clothing. The craft's popularity waned, but styles cycle. Now, macramé is resuming as artists create fresh patterns for the traditional knotting method. With the emergence of macramé in the 1970s, ornate rope work became common, appearing as tassels, placemats, and plant hammocks in room corners, picture frames, hammocks, wall hangings, and bikinis. With more buildings and trees being cut down, apartment people find macramé intriguing since it can turn hanging house plants into an alternative to a yard and a way to bring the outside in. This ancient practice has risen and fallen in popularity for thousands of years. This beneficial method will continue eternally. Fingers and a few simple tools can make table runners and key chains. Macrame must have one knot. Most Macrame is knotted. Sometimes Macrame is mixed with weaving or knitting to give a distinctive aesthetic.

Macramé needs hands and fingers. It may make plant hangers, apparel, wall art, dream catchers, jewelry, bracelets, pendants, curtains, tablecloths, placemats, tassels, keychains, bookmarks, and belts. Potential is endless. Beads, charms, and seashells may adorn your things. Once you master macramé's basic knots, you may go on to more sophisticated knots or create your own. You may use thick and colorful cables. Leather strips, linen rope, yarn, cotton, ribbon, nylon cable, and hemp cord are available. Hence Macramé is a traditionally feminine fiber art that fascinated women who valued personal growth and self-care. This book will help you make simple Macramé crafts quickly.

Chapter 1: The Beginnings of Macrame

A macrame is a type of knot that may be tied during the handcrafting process to create several different materials. Since the craft of macrame has gained recognition over the years, imaginative crafters and artists have developed innovative new applications for the material. These novel applications go beyond the usual uses of macrame, which include making plant hangers and wall hangings, among other things.

This age-old practice has had ebbs and flows of popularity for thousands of years. Nevertheless, because it is so applicable, this strategy will always be around in a certain form or the other. Amazingly, you only need your fingers and a few inexpensive components; you can make items like table runners and key chains.

Macrame is a technique for making textiles that involves tying many knots to create an object with a form and function that are fundamentally like the objects. The phrase "work not" is often used to allude to it. It is possible to use your hands to tie knots. To complete the job, you won't need further hardware to save a mounting clip.

Macrame is a term that can only be applied to a project if it includes at least each knot created using the beadwork technique. Macramé works are typically made by stringing together a series of knots to form the final product. Macrame pieces can sometimes be woven or stitched together along with elements that were created using other techniques, depending on the situation.

1.1: Where Macrame Got Its Start

Although knot-tying has been practiced for millennia, most experts believe that macramé only began within the last thousand years.

There are examples of knots being used as a method for record-keeping across the world, from the empire of the Incas in Latin America to Asia. Some of these examples are found in knots. For example, anglers used knots in ancient Greece to secure their fishing gear together. Knots were also employed for a variety of other useful uses.

The technique of tying beautiful knots has had a long and rich history as well; many of the knots employed in the past are being utilized now. For instance, the pan change knot has a long and illustrious history in China that dates to the Song Dynasty (950 to 1279 AD). This knot is just one of eight signs that reflect Buddhism and the idea that existence is a loop that doesn't have a start or an end. Other symbols include the lotus flower, the buddha, and the dharma wheel. It is also sometimes known as a butterfly's tie or a mystical knot, and it is believed that those who use it will be bestowed with good fortune throughout their lives.

Macramé, in the way we understand it today, did not begin till the 1300s, when Arabic weavers began to tie superfluous threads just at the borders of fabrics. Although humans get a long history of making knots, most experts think that macramé, in the sense that we know it now, did not start until that time. You may get a sense of what these plain knotted fringes looked like in their natural shape by looking at Turkish towels, which are still commonly used today. There is a large market for Turkish towels.

What began as a hobby that may be beneficial rapidly turned into an opportunity for embellishment, evolving straightforward utilitarian knots into its art form.

During the Moorish invasion of the Iberian Peninsula, which began in the ninth and lasted for several centuries, Arabic habits found their way to Europe, initially through Spain and then through France. This migration took place in the aftermath of the Moorish invasion. The women and slaves of warriors who traveled to the Middle East during the Crusades were exposed to the craft of macramé, which they brought back to Europe with them. Macramé became especially popular in Italy, notably in the city of Genoa. Because of these ladies, macramé began to gain traction in the Italian market.

Nuns in Europe, who had historically been skilled in needlework and lacemaking and utilized their skills to make stuff that was sold and utilized by the Church, were fast to see the benefits of this recently developed kind of artisanship. This was because nuns made things that were sold and employed by the Church. Because it was so simple to manufacture, macramé offered a less time-consuming and more straightforward alternative to the labor-intensive techniques of lacemaking that were prevalent during that era. They created wonderful, knotted lace that was quite popular and could be used for clothes or linens by proposing finer material instead of the conventional use of thick wool. This allowed the lace to be applied to clothes or linens. These ornamental panels might be sewn into garments or embroidered onto bed linens. Examples of their artwork may be found in locations such as paintings and costumes used in religious events. These are ideal places to search.

1.2: Macrame without the Use of Tools

The enormous popularity of macramé is not just attributable to the work of women or even the church, nor is it the sole craft about which people have sought unique and imaginative uses.

Macramé is a technique that was made popular by sailors. Sailors utilized the same basic knots as macramé, although they frequently referred to them by other names. Macramé is a technique that sailors popularized. Sailors were required to possess a working knowledge of knots because they spent their whole lives at sea. Macramé, also referred to as squared knotting, beautiful work, or McNamara's Lace, is a craft that sailors traditionally practiced combatting boredom when they were at sea for lengthy periods. When sailors returned to land, the one-of-a-kind items they had crafted gave them something to barter with. Furthermore, given the high regard in which information related to knots was held, sailors might even trade methods for tying knots with one another because this information was considered great value.

By bringing examples of their work to other ports throughout the globe, sailors were instrumental in the spread of the popularity of this handicraft. After it was brought to that region, it underwent further development and was frequently given various names, like Mexican lace.

A Powerful and Intense Reminiscence of the Victorian Period

In the second part of 19th century, Victorian households breathed new life into the dying art of macramé by incorporating it into their interior decor. During that period, the intricate detail of macramé, which resembles lace, was often worked into textiles such as linens, cloaks, and curtains. This was because macramé blended perfectly with the excessive interior décor of both the century, which may look cramped and crammed to the eyes of those living in the present day. The success of macramé was not just attributable to the attractiveness of the art form. When women of something like the middle class were expected to keep themselves engaged with handicrafts as just a necessary element of household life, macramé was a tempting alternative that offered a way to get around this expectation. Macramé is a reasonably easy style of needlework compared to other types of needlework, which is one reason it became popular at the time. Because it included the essential repetition of a few fundamental knots, macramé made it easier for women to complete their home tasks and explore creative handicrafts. This made it an appealing option for women. Macramé was also simpler to learn and become proficient at than other methods that generated equally appealing and desirable results.

Publications like "Sylvia's Book of Macramé Lace," released in 1890, offering even more women the confidence to take knots attempting to tie into their hands by telling them how and where to construct macramé for several products, including umbrellas, bags, clothes, and curtains. This allowed women to make their macramé for a wider range of items, which allowed them to save money. This growth was also influenced by the printing explosion that occurred concurrently with the Industrial Revolution.

In the end, macramé's popularity waned due to people's tastes shifting and larger cultural events impacting creative activities and arts and crafts. For instance, as more women entered the workforce, there was a gradual change away from seeing crafts as a vital component of daily life in the house. This was because more women were working outside the home. During the war, when there was a lack of resources, individuals resorted to crafts that were more "useful," including knitting and sewing. Examples include these phrases.

1.3: The Beginning of Contemporary Macrame

When and if macramé is once more pushed to the forefront of popular culture, you can bet that it will stir up quite a bit of controversy. As a result of the love children of the mid-1960s popularizing the art, macramé developed into a symbol of anti-industrialism within the larger counterculture movement. This was a result of the love of children's influence. Macramé was used by hippies not only to communicate their innovative thinking but a painting through which they could convey such drastic sentiments as just a protest the capitalist system and mass production. Hippies have been using it to communicate with their innovative thinking and painting. Crafts done by hand were one form of resistance that hippies employed against the capitalist system or mass manufacturing. Macramé blossomed into a bold and noisy art form, becoming famous in furniture decorating and the fashion industry. Macramé is a technique that uses a series of knots to create a fabric. The beautiful doilies that the macramé artists' ancestors had produced were not like the creations that the macramé artists created. It is reasonable to assume that macramé was used to adorn anything that may be embellished with it.

Due to the widespread exposure that macramé received, it rapidly spread to various facets of society and, as a result, it developed into a popular pastime that is now taught to youngsters. At some point, macramé began to find its way into the homes and wardrobes of "regular" people—those who weren't part of the larger counterculture movement.

Even while the over-the-top aesthetic of the 1970s, with its invasion of handmade monster wall hangings, eventually became outmoded, macramé has never completely gone out of favor. Instead, it has maintained a steady level of popularity. Nowadays, the normally envious images commonplace on social networking platforms may be given a more friendly and approachable atmosphere by using macramé curtains or plant hangers. This fashion is especially well-liked in the world of interior design.

Even though contemporary practitioners of macramé employ the same tangles and methods deployed by monarchs, sailors, and Victorians, those practitioners continue to develop new ways to have the channel represent the current period. For instance, they manufacture various goods, such as boho-chic clothing, luxury bags, ultra-modern jewelry, and home décor.

Currently of continual connectedness, the art of macramé has emerged to unwind, disconnect from technology, and focus on one's well-being. Because of this, people can now alleviate the strains of contemporary life while simultaneously engaging in activities that allow them to take their time and be creative.

Macramé is still practiced today as a reflection of the limitless ways a single material may be reinterpreted. Finding new and interesting ways to put one's spin on a practice that goes back hundreds or even thousands of years has never been easier than it is now. Macramé is an art form with a long and illustrious history of learning, and its skills have been adopted/passed down from generation to generation.

1.4: Some Advantages of Using Macrame

As with other types of handicrafts, macramé provides its practitioners with several advantages, among which are follows:

A Decrease in Stress and an Enhancement in Mental Clarity

The act is macramé has a soothing effect on the consciousness of the person doing it. When one can concentrate on the work, they are more likely to experience pleasant sensations and a sense of calm. The movements and postures that must be adopted to complete the practice create an environment suitable for meditation. You start to "tune out" the stressful and unpleasant sensations and substitute them with good thoughts and energy. This leads to a reduction in the amount of attention you devote to them.

Abilities of a Brain That Are Improved

Making things with your hands, like macramé or other creative projects, engages both hemispheres of your brain, which raises your awareness of your ability to focus, think quickly, and learn new things. When we take in new information, our brains produce new neurons and enhance connections between the ones they already contain and other cells and sensors.

The Improvement of One's Self-Esteem and Confidence

After completing a task, you will notice a rise in your sense of pride in yourself and your self-assurance. You have every right to be inspired and satisfied with yourself for taking on challenging new endeavors, expanding your horizons intellectually, and producing remarkable works of art.

Improved Motor Skills

Utilizing your hands, learning different knotting patterns, and practicing those patterns may all help to strengthen the nerves in your hands, fingers, and arms. This can be accomplished by utilizing your hands. Your natural ability improves, and with time, so does the pace with which you can carry out the necessary tasks. In addition, it is beneficial to the body, especially for those with a history of physical trauma, such as injuries or diseases. Crafting with young children helps them improve their motor abilities, enabling them to execute other tasks, such as reading, more easily.

The development of new capabilities

Macrame is not just an aesthetic endeavor; it also has practical applications. It has a high value in terms of its application since it enables one to create items that one may use, give presents, or sell. You may dig yourself out of a jam when times are bad, and money is tight by improving your talents and generating professional quality items.

It Creates an Exciting and Challenging Obstacle Course

Being indoors for lengthy periods may make you feel bored. The production of art and handicrafts may ease these sentiments while also confronting your body and brain with new difficulties. Practice is the only way to improve at macramé, a skill that can be developed endlessly. You start as a beginner, and as your 'level up,' you'll be able to construct patterns with increased intricacy. Getting to these professional levels is not a straightforward task, and to get there, you will need to consistently try new things, improve your skills, and practice.

Chapter 2: Macrame Terminologies

Reading designs for a project might be quite confusing when you are first starting, but it will become much less difficult as you get more expertise. It is impossible to figure out what kind of string one should buy without help. The following is a list of 19 terms about Macrame that every beginner need to be acquainted with. Exactly what does the term "sinnet" mean? Which method is more desirable, braiding or twisting the hair? When all we need to do is generate gorgeous fiber artwork that should be enough to get your mind to spin out of control. Let's get started by investigating the hidden meanings behind the macrame thread. Several varieties of string, cable, and rope are available. There are three primary categories of materials, and the one you decide to use for your project should be selected based on the look you want it to have at the end.

Macrame String: It is typically constructed from cotton, has a single twist, and is known for its exceptionally comfortable texture. It will produce a lovely fringe that is perfect for use in wall hangings and other ornamental applications. Because it is not very forgiving when redoing anything, you need to exercise caution if you need to undo and knot it several times.

Macrame Rope: It will be constructed out of three strands of cotton that have been twisted together. Although it is more robust than thread and not quite as soft, it is an excellent material for constructing plant hangers. The rope is the material I would recommend using for this task since it is easy to undo and re-tie, maintains its shape nicely when fringed, and gives the illusion of wavering.

Macrame Cable: It is normally constructed using six individual strands that are then braided together. Cotton or polypropylene, amongst other materials, could be used in the construction of it (plastic). Because it is so durable, a cord is an excellent choice as a building material for structures that need to be able to bear weight. Think about hanging your clothing on a clothesline. Most of the time, it fails to fringe correctly and ends up seeming rather fuzzy.

Now that the mystery has been solved let's talk about some terminology that will assist you in understanding a macrame design without making you feel like you're reading a foreign language.

LHK is an abbreviation for "lark's head knot". A thread loop creates a lark's head knot, securing the rope around the item. Additionally, it is used to join two separate strands of rope. Remember that the looping should be done at the front. It may be done by winding the rope around the dowel rod appropriately.

RLHK, also known as a reverse lark's head knot, is a kind of lark's head knot. The same as what was discussed before, but in the other way. The inverted lark's head knot is created by repeatedly looping the rope around the wooden rod in the opposite direction of the first loop.

HSK stands for "half square knot," which is an acronym for the term. The letter L illustrates the square knot's leftmost edge in this diagram. When you complete the HSK knots in a row, you will end up with a pattern that resembles a spiral.

RHSK stands for "right half squared knot," an acronym for the full term. On the other hand, this is not how the HSK works. When you have finished tying all the RHSK together, you will have a spiral pattern.

SK stands for "square knot," which may also be abbreviated as "SK." Putting together a half-squared knot and a right half-square knot results in forming a complete square knot. You will be tying square knots in each piece of jewelry you handcraft. You won't find a simpler or more fundamental knot than this one to learn how to tie.

HHK – also known as a half hook knot (also known as half hitch tying). A half-hook knot can significantly reduce the time & effort required to establish borders or limits. Depending on personal preference, this knot may also be tied on the right or left side of the body. Because an HHK is usually built-in pairs, the abbreviation DHHK will be used nearly all the time in patterns. This is because an HHK is nearly always built-in pairs. It is also overly critical/crucial to realize that an HHK may be linked vertically or horizontally; hence, you could hear the acronyms VHHK and HHHK used to refer to these types of connections, respectively. Are you at a stage where you do not understand anything?

ASK: Create alternating square knots in a circle. When creating ASKs, you must take half of the cords from the knots close by and tie a new knot to rest below and between the knots initially made.

Sinnet - A sinnet is a row of knots that are all the same and are organized in a column. Square knots are the conventional knot used while making a sinnet, a series of knots.

Working chords In the art of macramé, working chords refer to any of the cords used in the process.

Knotting cords — These cords are also the cords that are being used to tie the knots into your design. Knotting cords come in a range of colors and are available for purchase.

Filler cords are tied around knots in your craft to make it look complete. Filler cords are also known as finishing cords.

A row is a continuous stripe of knots tied next to one another and knotted with a different workplace thread than the knots that came before them in the row. A finishing knot is tied at each end of the cords used to bind them. This is done to prevent the cords from unraveling. The HHK motif is completed on these hardwood handbags handles with a simple knot that stops the design from unraveling and pulls it closer together.

A gathering knot is used either at the commencing or at the end of a project to unite and secure the many cords. A plant hanger's beginning and end are often finished with a gathering knot since this type is particularly efficient. After you've understood these macrame terms, you'll be up to speed and ready to interpret a macrame pattern.

Depending on your choice, macramé may be manufactured using various synthetic fibers. For most conventional applications, you will need cords with a thickness ranging from 3 millimeters up to 6 millimeters. A method known as micro-macramé may be used to produce jewelry and other small decorative items. Simply put, it refers to using a string with a thickness ranging from 0.5 mm to 2 mm.

Chapter 3: Tools and Materials

When it relates to macramé, it takes more than just your hands and some rope to get the job done. There is a process, an art, and, most importantly, helpful instruments that you can use to construct various outstanding macrame projects.

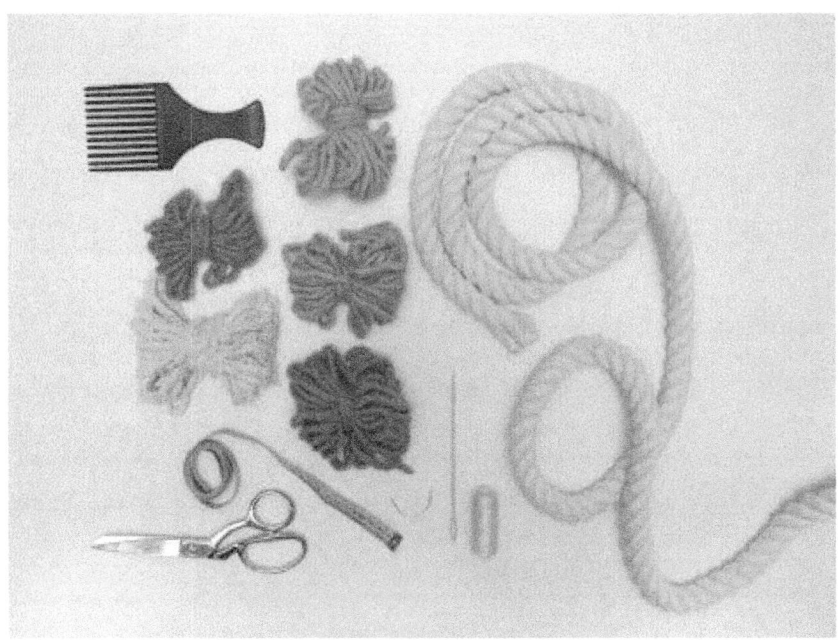

You can use these things to your advantage. You can combine a collection of the most helpful instruments to create stunning macrame creations. Some among them are necessities, while others are only nice-to-haves, but it all depends on the activities most appeal to you. It is vital to understand essential macrame tools to use them effectively, and for the purpose, they were designed. As soon as you have acquired the knowledge necessary to effectively apply the appropriate tools, you will be able to discriminate between them and apply each to your work to achieve better outcomes.

3.1: Project Board

Compatible with various string applications such as decorative knotting, Macramé, and producing jewelry. When working on tiny products, such as bookmarks or jewelry, this tool comes in helpful. Because of the notches that are strategically placed on all four sides, your rope will be held in place securely, and you won't need to use any pins. These boards, made of lightweight material, are easily transportable and can go with you wherever you go. There are two different sizes available for the Macrame Boards: The mini macrame board measures 6 inches by 9 inches (15 cm by 23 cm), making it ideal for micro-macrame. The large macrame board measures 14 inches by 10 inches (36 x 25 cm). Macramé project board that is lightweight and has a surface that can mend itself. While working on a project, a cable can be held firmly in place with the assistance of a notched edge on all four sides. It enables you to tie knots that are even while you are working. The grid format is labeled with both centimeters and inches to facilitate measurement. These specifically crafted Macramé Panels are a play since they provide you with a flat, movable cutting board for your projects. In addition, they come with both the metric and imperial dimensions printed on them. You won't have to worry about balancing your creations on your knees, using clothes pins or tape to hold your work, or looking for a ruler again! This carefully designed macramé board measures 290 millimeters by 400 millimeters and is made from wood that can mend itself, making it better for the environment over plastic or foamy boards. For all significant macramé project requirements, each board features a double-sided line graph with both imperial and metric measurements measurement markings. It is covered by a cover that can be wiped clean (but you should not remove it!).

When it comes to macramé, the most critical piece of equipment to have been a design mounting board. The work is done on this board, which serves as the working surface on which screws or other fasteners are used to hold the work in place. The fronts of the boards sold in craft stores often have grid-inch marks and size suggestions, and these boards may be used for various crafts. On the other hand, a project board may be made by either utilizing cork or foam sheets that have been glued together. If the board is sufficiently thick, it may be used for a macramé project; this is provided, of course, that the pins cannot be seen poking out from below the board's surface.

3.2: T-Pins

These specifically crafted Macramé Boards are a significant change since they provide you with a flat and portable workpiece surface for your projects. In addition, they come with both the metric and imperial dimensions printed on them. You won't have to worry about balancing your projects across your knees, using clothes pins or tape to hold your work, or looking for a ruler again! These metal T-Pins from Beads MTh are ideal for welding, in addition to having a variety of applications in Macrame, segments and sub, and other crafts that require high-quality steel T-Pins. You can get them here. They are also quite useful for soldering since they are ideal for holding little works upright while the solder is now being applied. This makes them a very convenient tool for use in this process. They have a length of 43 millimeters and were designed specifically for use with a Macrame Panel, Soldering Board, or any other craft application that calls for a sturdy, strong, and high-quality holding T pin. Both boards can be purchased elsewhere at James's Place. T-pins are made of metal that can be used in conjunction with macramé creating boards. When working on macramé creations, pins or boards can simplify connection management, which is especially helpful for more complicated designs. These pins have a length of 51 millimeters and a thickness of 1.2 millimeters. It's essential to thread the wire through to the lace project's edges, and then you will need to secure the wires by inserting pins along the interior of the wires while the lace dries. T-pins have a wide variety of applications, the most common of which is to fasten a piece of fabric or materials to a solid surface. Each T-Pin has a head in the shape of a T-Bar and an extremely sharp point, allowing it to pierce even the most complex surfaces without breaking or breaking.

3.3: Patterns

Macrame is not an art form that should be associated with the 1970s, and thanks to the tremendous success of the craft's recent comeback, we're getting in on the action too! Since the crafts and abilities involved in macramé lend themselves perfectly to our incredibly adaptable elastic bands, it would be a good idea to go all out and enhance a variety of colored cords, dowels, and beads to our collection so that you can shop for everything you need for macramé in one location. Look at our newly stocked assortment of macrame items, read up on some of the fundamentals of the craft, and get to know some of the most talented macrame lampshade manufacturers around. Make a traditional plant hanging out of Macrame that you can use indoors or outdoors. It is a design that has continued the test of time, even though it uses its bailing twine to build the hoop from which it will hang. Macrame wall hangings are a stylish way to show off your knotting talents, and this pattern and guide will allow you to do that. This macrame pattern is for a laptop mat, but it may just as quickly be used to make a placemat, tiny table runners, or even a trivet. It creates an elaborate pattern by tying three knots: a square, a horizontal halfway hitch, and a diagonal half hitch.

This beautiful macrame necklace may be made if you have some leather lace, thread, and fabric dye. Modify the look of this simple project that can be completed in an afternoon by altering the dye's color or leaving its residuals for a more bohemian appearance. This enormous macrame rope light will help you make a bold statement. Every room in our house will benefit from the unexpected element that it brings! To create this one-of-a-kind macrame artwork, you will need a cording, a lamp chord, and a socket kit. With the same free macrame trivet template, you can give your dining area or kitchen a dash of the sleek and modern Scandinavian design aesthetic. A wooden stitching hoop and a few drops are all you need to construct this trivet, which makes it an inexpensive craft project that doesn't skimp on design. Using this free macrame design for giant feathers, you can create a wall exhibit that will have your friends green with envy. It would not take much effort to adapt the pattern so that it could be used to create miniature feathers that may be used as ornaments or even keychains. Get yourself a pair of hoop earrings and some macrame cord, and you'll be all set to create these gorgeous earrings. You will have a brand-new pair of earrings in a little over half an hour if you follow the straightforward instructions.

3.4: Scissors

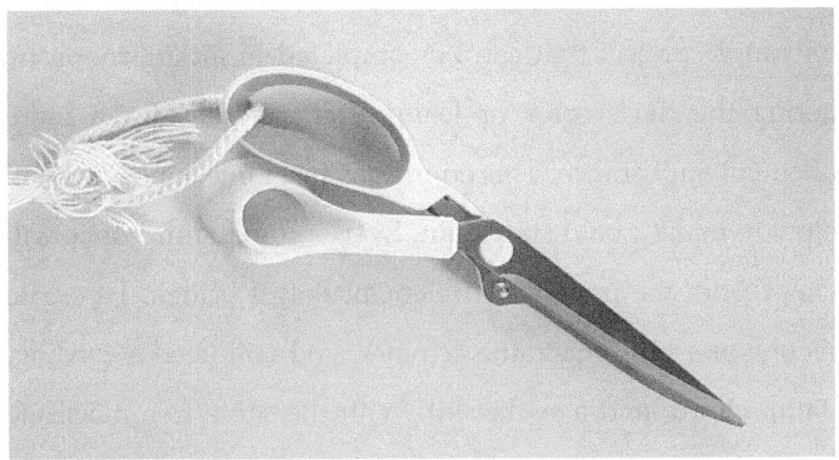

The blades & handles of these super-sharp scissors were made of recycled materials to save resources. These are an essential component of your macrame toolset since they allow you to cut crisp, straight lines and ends precisely and neatly in your macrame creations. For any textile craft, having very sharp scissors is essential. It's just one of that stuff that, if you have sharp scissors, you don't even think about, but if you don't, it becomes VERY evident very quickly.

Cutting the ideal fringed on your macrame products if you have dull scissors will be a pain. When creating stunning works of fiber art with Macrame, you do not require a lot of different equipment, but you need sharp scissors. The most common cutting tool used for Macrame is a pair of scissors. When cutting macramé with scissors, you should spend your money on a high-quality rather than a cheap pair. When using a pair of scissors of higher quality, cutting fringe is not only considerably simpler but also more fun. It's like comparing day and night. Now that you're using scissors of higher quality, you need to be more conscientious about how you care for them. You can observe the following guidelines: Take care not to drop them. On Reddit, some manufacturers recommended having them sharpened by an expert or bringing them to Ginger to be sharpened. Keep things in the sheathing if it comes with one; if it does not, do not keep them.

Macramé scissors are an outstanding pair of sharp scissors

that can cut threads on a macramé project accurately and precisely. You may use these scissors to make macramé necklaces, bracelets, and other items. For your convenience, a wide selection of grips are available in several sizes. It is recommended that you get a model with sheath protection to ensure the safety of the blades.

Because you will be cutting and clipping threads as you sew on your Macrame masterpiece, I recommend getting an excellent pair of sharp scissors. I can't say enough decent things about the stunning vintage embroidery scissors that can be purchased at BIHRTC. These pointed edges craft scissors are well regarded for their ergonomic metal handle and razor-sharp blades, which enable you to cut cords more accurately than you would be able to do with other types of craft scissors. The Living Premium Tailor Scissors and the Fiskars Amplify Scissors are fantastic options for a bigger pair of shears. These dressmaker scissors are constructed for cutting through tough textiles, making them an excellent choice for use in macramé work.

3.5: Precision Tweezers

Macramé is an old form of weaving that originated in Arabia and is used to create colorful fringes for veils, shawls, and bath towels, among other things. This knotting method produces belts, wall hangings, plant hangers, and jewelry. With enough experience, it is possible to create elaborate one-of-a-kind masterpieces. To get started with macramé, you will need a few simple and affordable pieces of equipment. Tweezers are another item that comes in handy when working on decorative projects. Tweezers can be helpful when knotting tiny threads in between beadwork because of their precision. When you want to unwind knots or adjust your work, precise tweezers are the tool that will serve you best. This prevents any harm to the wires and makes it much simpler to remedy any errors that may have been made.

3.6: Rotary Cutter

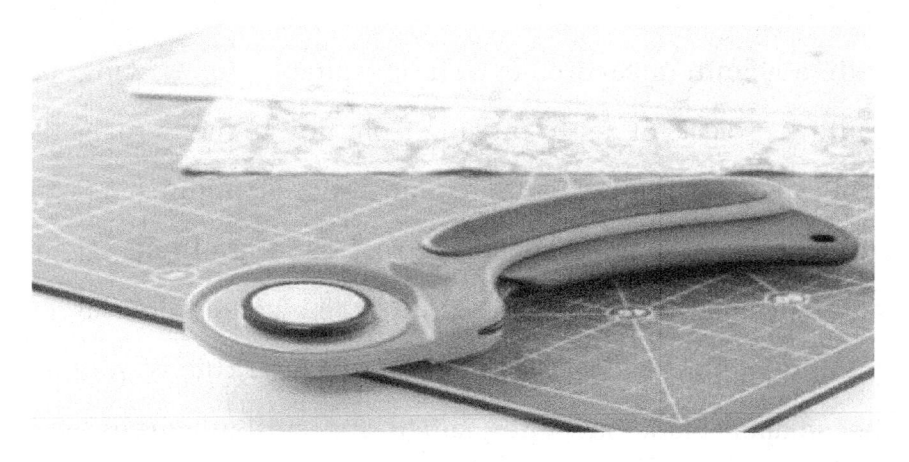

A rotary cutter, to put it in the simplest, most direct terms possible. When first learning how to operate a rotary cutter, it is not always easy to make "clear-cut" decisions regarding which brand to purchase because there are various brands available, not to mention a variety of shapes and sizes. Consider the benefits the cutter will provide you and the number of uses that can be found for this helpful item. A rotary cut is equipment used for cutting cloth and craft materials.

It has a handle device and an extremely sharp round blade. Because the blade spins, you'll be able to cut more quickly and accurately than ever before. They are available in various designs, handle configurations, and sizes. All the blades, no matter what size they are (18 mm, 28 mm, 45 mm, or 60 mm), come equipped with a lock so that the forefront is never exposed. 45mm and 60mm are the sizes that are utilized the most frequently. You will most frequently come across blades with a 45mm measurement. It is suitable for sewing or quilting projects of a size ranging from tiny to medium, as its name suggests. A blade with a diameter of 60 millimeters can cut through more significant projects and multiple layers simultaneously. Most of the time, it is utilized for larger quilting jobs instead of sewing apparel. As a rule of thumb, the smaller blade is better suited for cutting curves and corners, while the larger blade, as one might expect, can handle a more significant amount of fabric at once. If you want the most remarkable outcomes and to reduce the risk of accidents, you should make every effort to use the appropriate blade for the job. You may need even more least 1 size of cutter, depending on the kinds of things you sew daily.

You are probably looking for a practical tool to help you cut the macramé cords more precisely. You should use a Rotary Cutter! Utilizing a rotary cutter will make cutting feathers and fringes much quicker and easier. I like using the Fiskars Rotary Crafts Cutter with this eco-friendly self-healing slicing mat because it allows me to do the task promptly and effectively.

3.7: Crochet Hooks

Knitting's close relative, crochet, is a needlework technique in which the artist creates various objects by knitting together threads of yarn with crochet hooks. The patterns for popular crocheted items such as mittens, potholders, and sometimes even jumpers and headbands can be learned by anybody interested in the craft. Since the beginning of time, maybe even a century ago, crochet has been a popular technique to produce various garments. Crochet within the realm of needlework can reflect a long and illustrious history. The word "crochet" derives from the French term for "hook," which refers to the wing needle that makes it possible to crochet. Crochet is thought to have originated in the 1600s out of earlier types of fibrecraft. Before this, however, there are examples from what would later become contemporary crochet that may be dated far further to the embroidery of ancient China. The primary step in manufacturing crochet is "looping," which involves wrapping the yarn around the and using hooks to pinch, pull, and otherwise manipulate the thread. This is quite like knitting, but it is quite different from Macrame, which would be made by knotting the rope together and creating a pattern. One more of the most significant distinctions between crochet and Macrame is that handmade projects always require the same quantity of yarn from the beginning to the end of the process. In contrast hand, a macrame project requires several lengths of cord or rope, all of which must be knotted together to finish the project.

3.8: Corkboard

Corkboards are ideal for macramé because you can fasten your work with pins, which is particularly helpful when working on smaller projects like macramé jewelry or a macramé pocketbook. Even though any bulletin board will work, the one covered in plastic is the best option for macrame projects since it eliminates the possibility of cork dust getting into the finished product. For intricate designs involving knotting and braiding, the Macramé Board will significantly assist. Cork with half an inch (12.7 mm) is covered in paper with a grid of one inch (25.4 mm) for quick and accurate measurements. The board is sent to you in a plastic sleeve, which helps with projects requiring tape and ensures that the paper stays attached to the corkboard. The board has dimensions of 11 inches by 17 inches (28 centimeters by 43 centimeters) and comes with five to six steel t-pins measuring 1.5 inches long (38 millimeters). Even when the macramé project board does not have a self-healing feature, if it is used consistently, it should be able to supply the crafter with many years of quality assistance.

In addition, corkboards are great for macramé since they enable you to connect your work with pins. This feature is especially helpful when working on smaller pieces like macramé jewelry or a macramé purse. Corkboards are available at craft stores and online. If you need/want to be sure that your finished macrame projects do not have any trace of cork in them, it is best to use a corkboard that has been wrapped in plastic, even though you may use any corkboard for this purpose. These T-pins and helpful instructions are pre-printed on the front of this Macrame-specific corkboard, designed exclusively for use in Macrame crafts.

3.9: Macrame Rope

Macramé cords are created by weaving together several threads in a particular pattern. After that, they are twisted together continuously to form an extra smooth and even fiber with no fishbones (fishbones are the thread that is out of place in a cable). This method is repetitive until there are no fishbones present. A cord is typically considerably smoother and softer than rope, giving your item an appearance free of odd twists and knots. When deciding on the best macramé cord for your project, you should consider whether you want to work with natural or synthetic fibers. This is because both types of fibers have their benefits and drawbacks. The most common choices include materials made from natural fibers such as cotton, hemp, bed sheets, bamboo, jute, and wool. These materials are not harmful to the environment, as they are sustainable, biodegradable, easily accessible, and inexpensive. Manufactured solid and long-lasting fibers include polypropylene, microfiber, acrylic, rayon, paracord, and plastic. Synthetic fibers also include plastic. They are an excellent choice for projects that take place outside and require high resistance to weather effects. Cotton and hemp are not as plush and cozy as wool or cashmere, even though they might have a relatively soft feel to the touch.

3.10: Cotton String

The string is comparable to a rope; the primary distinction between the two is that string is not plied like a rope. Instead, it is made up of a significant number of fragile threads that are contorted together to form a single strand. You can also come across the term "single-strand macrame rope" when searching for this cable. Because of how it is constructed, it is considerably more pliable than macrame ropes, resulting in more compact and secure knots. It is also far more likely to expand and have an uneven thickness, so you shouldn't be surprised if it is 1 mm larger or smaller than advertised. Despite this, it's simple to fringe, and the finished product gives larger projects a beautiful, supple look. In contrast, three-ply rope tends to produce fringe with a wave-like pattern. This fringe is delicate and straight. Macrame string with a diameter of 6 millimeters is ideal for use in projects that do not hold weight, making it an excellent choice for novices. Just keep an eye on it to ensure it doesn't start unraveling in the center of your piece!

3.11: Embroidery Floss

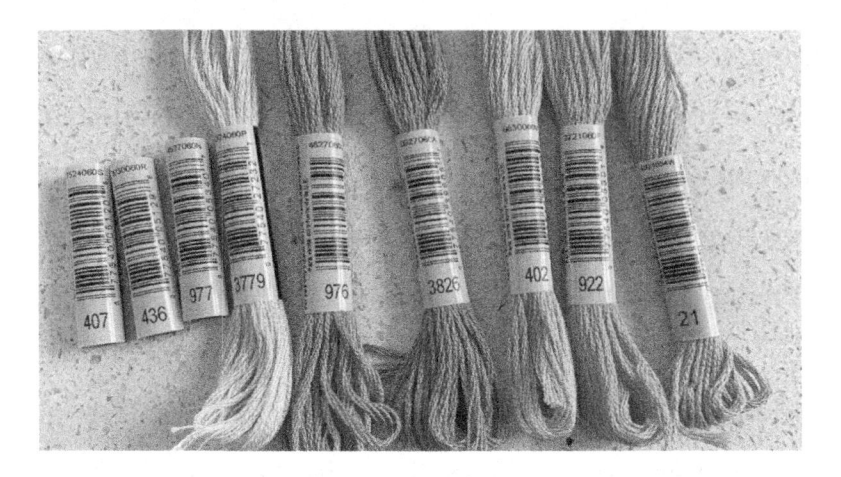

Textile, silk, and rayon have traditionally been the materials that are used to manufacture embroidery floss. However, rayon has always been considered the highest sheen of the three. Since it is more difficult to find and a more recent addition to a specific product line, linen floss is in higher demand to produce historically accurate period costumes. Embroidery floss can be purchased in many plain colors, and many fibers can also be purchased in varied color options. Floss with a Novelty. In addition to being offered in various fibers, embroidery floss, much like knitting yarn, also features a wide selection of novelty options. One example is metallic floss, which consists of metallic fibers mixed with viscose. However, as another example, you can also purchase fluorescent and glow-in-the-dark floss varieties.

Chapter 4: Principal and Useful Knots

Macrame is a craft manufacturing process that involves tying knots into thread or cords to form a geometric pattern for many ornamental objects, including textiles. This design may be used for a variety of decorative purposes. In another sense, it may be described as tying decorative knots in one's hands. A mounting ring is the only equipment required to keep the item in place while operations are performed. Macramé can be utilized in manufacturing a broad variety of things, such as jewelry, purses, and even pieces of clothing. Macramé plant pots and macramé wall hangings are just two examples of the enormous range of products that can be made using this technique. Low-cost materials like cotton thread, hemp, or yarn may be used to make useful and aesthetically beautiful products. This is possible because of the versatility of these materials. In recent years, the usage of macrame has grown beyond its traditional functions as a plant catcher and as a type of wall art, which has contributed to the popularity of this art form. Macrame has been practiced in various innovative and creative ways by artists and crafters in recent years.

Utilize the resources you already have for your early creative endeavors to save costs. If you want to avoid wasting substantial cash on an activity, it could be good if you knew that you would like to participate. Choose any thread from the available list and any rings used for fastening things. Look around your house for a piece of furniture or a plank that you can use as a makeshift desk throughout the day. You may prevent your string from sliding off the board by using macrame pegs, which are available for purchase online. On the other hand, to save expenses and make your initial attempt more manageable, you may utilize safety pins.

4.1: Lark's Head Knot

The Lark's Head Knot is widely considered one of the most effective knots for affixing macramé threads to something like a rod or ring.

- Create a loop with one macramé cord by folding it in half lengthwise.
- Place the folded wire on the work area with the loop points in the other direction so that the ends of the cord are facing upward.

- It would help if you positioned your rod (or ring) on the folded rope directly above the loop. To secure it in place, you should use a nut.

- Wrapping the cord around the dowel will ensure its stability (or ring).

- To pull everything together more tightly, bring the ends of the rope up, feed them into the loop, and then let them fall back down.

4.2: The Cow Knot

The Reversed Lark's Headed knot, also known as the Cow Knot Tie, is what Lark's Heads braid looks like when seen from the other side. The Lark's Heads braid is also known as Lark's Heads braid. The choice between Lark's Head and the Reverse Lark's Head knots is up to personal preference because of the apparent similarity between the two.

- Folding a single macramé strand in half along its length is necessary.

- Place the folded rope on the surface of the work area so that the loop is pointing upward, and its ends are pointing downward.

- Place the rod (and ring), then secure it with a nut, over the folding cord, right above where the loop is located.

- Place the loop around the shaft in a downward direction (or ring).

- To pull everything together more tightly, you should first drag the ends of the rope up and then into the loop until bringing them back down.

4.3: A Knot Tied in Half

In most cases, the construction of a sinnet (take notice of the peculiar name!) starts with tying half knots. When tied together, half knots produce a natural spiral often seen in handcrafted plant-hanging accessories. To finish Half Knot, you will need to work with four cords. The knot-bearing cords and the knotting wires each consist of two cords positioned on each side of the knotting cords.

- After passing the left plaiting cord underneath the right braided rope cord and through the twin lace cords, bring a left-braided rope thread to the right.

- Bring the cord of the right braid rope below the two twisted strands on the left, and then cross it over the cord used to tie the knot on the left.

- To make the knot further/more secure, bring the ropes

used to tie it closer together.

4.4: Square Knot

The Square Tie is an upgrade on the Half Knot in design and function. This can be said about the shape of the tie as well. In this context, "half of a square" refers to the entire square. To finish the square, first, you must tie the first midway knot just like any other, and then you must tie a second halfway tie using the strands opposite one another.

- To finish the Square Knot, follow the steps listed below.
- Bring the correct braid rope cord to the left, and then cross that right plaiting cord over twin lace cords and below the left plaiting cord.
- To tighten the center knotting cord properly, draw the left plaiting yarn to the left and across it. This will bring it

under the center knotting cord.

- To make the knotting cords more secure, bring them closer together.

4.5: The Knot Overhead

Before you even realized it had a name, you had probably tied these knots a hundred times before noticing it. It is useful for tying off the ends of braids or cords used as plant hangers.

- Create a loop by passing one(1) end of the rope over the other end of the rope.

- Bring the rope's top end behind the ring and up through it.

- To make the cable more secure, pull the ends of the cord closer to make the cable more secure.

4.6: The Spiral Stitch

Especially in more historically accurate designs, the working strands in a macramé project are often much longer than the filler cords. Since this is only a practice session, the duration of each one probably won't very much.

- Working chord 1 should be relocated to the left so it is below working chord 1 and over gaps (cords 2–3).

- Move the working wire 4 to the right to position it over cord 1 and below the fillers. Pull on both working threads while holding your fillers, so they are under tension when you want to strengthen a Half Knot.

- This step involves switching the orientation of the two working cords, but the subsequent Half Knot has been done similarly. Return to step 1 and transfer working cable 4 to the next position. Return to step 2, then relocate the functioning cable 1 to the new location.

- After moving the working cable to the LEFT, tie 3 half knots while maintaining the initial position of the working cord. While you work your way through the knots, squeeze them together. Turn the knots so that they face rightward to switch the places of the two operating wires. It is necessary to spin the spiral to guarantee that it maintains its uniformity over the whole of the sennit.

- Rotate again after making 5 more quarter knots on the rope. If you still have enough material, you should repeat the procedure.

4.7: The Clove Hitch

Is the beginning and ending knot in many lashings. You may tie it like this:

- Bring the free end of the rope over the pole and tuck it under it.

- Repeat the previous step of wrapping the ends around, this time forming an X by crossing one end over the other.

- In the third step, loop the end of the rope around and then tuck it under the X. The ends of the rope should be able to be seen emerging from within the X's legs. If they leave the X at any of the two opposite corners, you do not have a cloves hitch.

- To make the hitch more secure, bring the two ends of the rope closer together.

4.8: Chinese Knot

First, secures a rope measuring sixty inches to the middle of the board. The first loop is created by crossing that right half across to the left side.

- Turning the right-hand side of the wire counterclockwise produces loop 2, which may then be used. It should halt off to the side in loop 1 at some point.

- Slide circle 2 to the left and tuck it under the left side of Loop 1 to create three gaps between the two loops. Put the appropriate end of the cable onto your board

- The fourth step in this process is to move a rope to the left while simultaneously crossing its left side across its right side. It should be braided from left to right over, under, though, and under loops 1 and 2.

- Make a diagonal cut to the left down the length of the cord, which will allow you to cross both parts of loop 1 and the right shoulder of a cord with the left half of a cord. Move it down underneath the last two portions of cycles 2 or 3. After making certain that it is positioned towards the left of both the right side, secure it.

- This step involves passing the rope through circle 2 on both sides after first crossing the right half of the loop over the left half. Bring it down below the left edge of loop 1. The X in this illustration indicates the exact location of the knot's focal point.

- As you go down the right of both ropes to finish loop 5, you will need to cross the first three obstacles.

- It should travel through the center (the X), then rest below the three sections that came after it.

Chapter 5: Choosing Materials for Macrame

An ancient Arabian weaver's expertise that has been passed down the generations is the ability to create decorative fringes on veils, shawls, and bath towels. This technique has been used for thousands of years. Macramé is a type of knotting currently used to construct various items, including plant hangers, wall hangings, jewelry, and belts, among other things. You can make complicated one-of-a-kind goods if you have some prior knowledge in the field. To get started with macramé, you will need a few straightforward and inexpensive instruments.

Macramé may be used to create a stunning organic focal point in the décor of a space that might otherwise be boring or clinical. Macramé, which has been created, often has an organic form. This natural element may generate a feeling of tranquility that matches the contemporary minimalism employed to emphasize the accentuated item. Macramé is versatile enough to be utilized in various ways, including as a kind of art that may be displayed on a wall. Since they are generally handcrafted, they will impart an organic feel to the atmosphere you have created, and since they are one of a kind, they will serve as a possible conversation starter. Macramé may be displayed in any location, but a large wall that is otherwise devoid of decoration is where we suggest displaying it. You may create harmony in a space by ensuring that the item you choose (or the one you build yourself) compliments the aesthetics, items, forms, and aesthetic value of the space you work in. If you want to hang it on a huge wall that is vacant above a piece of wood, you should choose a larger macramé object with a broader breadth. Because of this, it will be able to occupy the area above the piece of furniture in a complementary and uncluttered manner. The fact that macramé is both organic and authentic adds to the charm of the craft. No one product can be considered the "standard" for macramé. Macrame has been an important trend for several years, and its popularity is projected to grow even more in 2021 and beyond. Have you ever considered learning how to become competent at Macrame? With the help of this convenient checklist, you'll be able to get started fast and tie some knots. Then, you'll be ready to make whatever macramé creations your heart could want! Keep reading to learn more about and receive suggestions on all the supplies you need to construct your first macrame project and learn more about Macrame in general!

Macramé is a kind of textile art that incorporates the process of making knots. It is a time-honored mode of creative expression that dates to the thirteenth century and is thought to have been invented by Arab weavers. This form of artistic expression may be traced back to weaving. These expert crafters made ornate fringes by making knots out of the excess thread and yarn along the borders of hand-loomed textiles like bath towels, blankets, and veils. Examples of these types of materials include veils, blankets, and bath towels. During the latter half/part of the 18th century, the courts of Mary II were responsible for bringing art to England. At this stage, it had already taken hold over all of Europe. It was common knowledge that Queen Mary taught her ladies-in-waiting the art of macramé throughout her reign.

In their spare time at sea, sailors made macramé products, which they would sell or barter once they arrived at the port. This way, the art form spread to other regions, including China and the Americas. Slings, bell fringes, and belts were some items that sailors from the United Kingdom and the United States used macramé to make throughout the nineteenth century. They called the process "square knotting," after the kind of knot they used. Most Sailors also called macramé "McNamara's Lace".

During the Victorian period, one of the most popular types of laceworks was macramé, crochet. It was used to embellish many objects, including sleeves, undergarments, drapes, and jewelry. The art of macramé was once quite popular, but it went out of shape for a spell there. However, it was not until the 1970s that it was once again popular to produce wall hangings, articles of apparel, bedspreads, small denim shorts, tablecloths, curtains, plant hangers, and other things used to decorate the house. You couldn't call yourself a genuine free spirit if you didn't know how to build a string handbag with macramé. That is, until it followed in the footsteps of platforms clad in velvet kaftans and disappeared into a pot of fondue, never to be seen or heard from again. By the early 1980s, macramé had already started to go out of favor, but in the last five years, the craft has been gradually making a resurgence. Macramé was once again falling out of favor by the early 1980s. By the early 1980s, macramé had fallen out of favor dramatically and was no longer widely used. The usage of contemporary Macrame is gaining popularity all over the globe, and a great part of this may be attributed to the proliferation of e-commerce websites & social media platforms like Instagram, Etsy, and Pinterest. This fad will not go away any time soon.

Rope, cable, string, and yarn are all products that may be

made from natural materials such as cotton, linens, hemp, jute, leather, and wool. These are wonderful for indoor projects, such as house decoration, art, accessories, gift wrapping, and textiles. Because they can be broken down by natural processes, using them in craft projects is an option that is gentler in the natural world. Examples of synthetic fibers include polypropylene, acrylic, nylon, and even plastic. Other examples include rayon and lyre. They are not susceptible to deterioration when exposed to the elements, making them good options for projects to be carried out in the open air since they are hardy in damp and dry environments. The rope is offered in a diverse selection of thicknesses and lengths, some of which are more suited for certain tasks than others. Ropes with a diameter of three millimeters or less are perfect for use in jewelry applications. Ropes with a diameter ranging from 4 millimeters to 7 millimeters are perhaps the ones that are used the most. These ropes are perfect for use in various applications, including plant hangers, tapestries, furniture, chandeliers, curtains, and carpets, among other things. Large ropes, with diameters ranging from 8 to 12 millimeters (and even greater), may be utilized to generate a visual expression and are a lot of fun to work with, particularly when producing wall hangings.

5.1: Tweezers for fine detail work & crochet hooks

Since crochet hooks enable you to pull your threads through minuscule loops without having to tie them together, they are a particularly beneficial tool when dealing with tiny cords and crafting macramé jewelry. Crochet hooks can be found at most craft stores. In addition, they come in helpful when it comes time to complete a piece of work, such as the bottom for the macrame bags you have made. When you need to unravel knots or get too few alterations to your work, your best choice is to use precise tweezers because of their pinpoint accuracy. Because of this, any potential damage to the wires is avoided, and it is much easier to correct any problems.

5.2: Needles

Needles are essential for the construction of the finished product and the application of beading and other decorations. Whether to use blunt-end or tapestry needles, Chenille needles, or pointed needles is ultimately up to the individual. Different diameters may accommodate a wide range of yarn types, including nylon and silk, as well as various bead shapes and styles.

5.3: Comb of Fringes

I recommend using a strong steel comb to unwind your threads to get the perfect fringe for the macramé project you are working on. Consider also using a specialized brush designed for pets since this is something that I've seen quite a few people use when they want to comb a fringe. When making feathers, if you want the fringe to be firm, using fabric stiffener spray is a technique that is highly suggested.

5.4: Macramé Bead Smith Board (Macramé Bead Board)

Because of their portability, Macrame Bead Smith Boards are useful for creating small crafts such as bookmarks and jewelry. Thanks to the specially created slots on both sides of the spool, your rope will remain securely in place without needing pins. Because the material used to make these boards is so lightweight, it is feasible to take them anywhere. The Macrame Bead Smith Boards are offered in two distinct sizes, which are as follows: There is a Mini Macrame Board that is 6 inches by 9 inches (15 x 23 cm) and is perfect for micro-macrame. A Large Macrame Board measures 14 inches by 10 inches (35 cm by 25 cm) and is perfect for large-scale Macrame (36 x 25 cm).

The Macrame Beads are frequently utilized for macramé projects constructed using materials measuring between 3mm and 8mm. In addition, there are some pointers on sizing, preparation, and various procedures. When shopping for beads for macramé, the hole size is the most crucial characteristic to pay attention to. In addition, you need to consider the breadth of the material, the number of cords that go through the beads, and how flexible the substance is. The beads' total size (length) will influence how they appear in your finished product. Beads that are large and hefty strung on thin ropes will not seem appealing. You need to strike a balance here between the size of the beads and the overall design of the thing you're making.

5.5: Tape

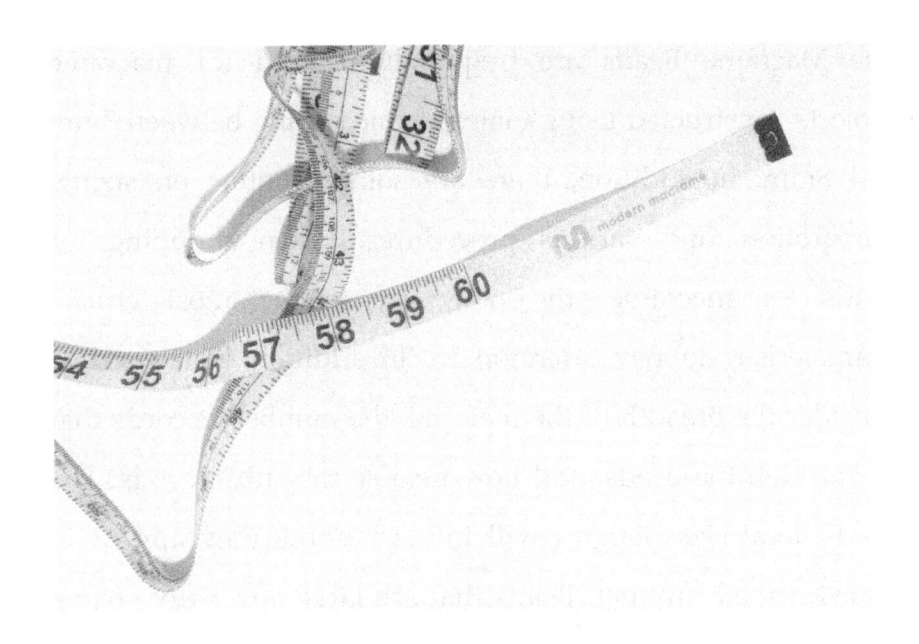

It is much easier to finish smaller projects like plant hangers and wall hangings if you tape the beginning of your project to a surface so that you can work from it. This makes it possible for you to work from it. If the knots on your project are not tied correctly, the rope will get tangled, and tugging on the knots will cause your craft to become disorganized and fly all over the place when you attempt to use it. One additional strategy I've tried and discovered helpful for large-scale tasks is putting them up on a hanger or hooks that you could already have in your home. I've found this to be an effective solution. If you have picture frames with curtains, you may hang your dowel from the hooks on the curtains and start working from that point! When brushing out the string used for your macramé birds and fringes, you will want to use a sturdy comb. Using a polyester comb is acceptable and capable of completing the task at hand; nevertheless, it is not as efficient as using a steel comb, and the quality of the work it produces will not be comparable. Utilize a steel comb for the most efficient and effective results. On the other hand, investing in a pet comb will save time and help you untangle any knots that may have accumulated along the way.

5.6: Shook

These essential elements must be included in the macramé wall hangings you are constructing. Investing in wooden dowels could be smart if you want the finished product to have an uncluttered and organized look. If on the other side, you want to achieve a more bohemian and rustic look, then tree branches or even driftwood will be a great alternative for you. When you go out on your next walk or spend some time by the lake, make it a point to keep an eye out for any pieces of driftwood or interesting tree branches that you may be able to bring back with you.

The Macrame board serves as the working surface, allowing you to grip and manage your project without risk of injury. If you so wish, you may purchase a Macrame board from an arts and crafts retailer. A store specializing in sewing and supplies is likely the best place to look for T-pins, also often referred to as "wig" pins. You might also consider buying U-pins, a good choice for fastening huge cords to the same macrame board. This is another alternative that you could investigate. You will need to use the crochet hook and the sewing needle for the tasks in which you are tasked with finishing off a rather complex macrame design with several specific tiny details. Once your list of macrame materials has been exhausted and you have acquired everything else you need, the only point left for you to do is to make Macrame. Beginning a new endeavor, such as Macrame, is often the most challenging part of the process. Use some free lessons and plans to get started if you're having difficulties getting started, and keep in mind that you can always start again if things aren't going how, you imagined they would. If you're having trouble getting started, use some free lessons, and plans to get started.

On the other hand, if you put in the time & effort necessary and put what you've learned into practice, you may become an expert in Macrame! You will need both to calculate the lengths of cable you will require for your project and the amount of wall space you will require for your macramé wall hangings. You will be notified of the lengths of cable you need, and there is nothing more unpleasant than running out of cords when making an elaborate pattern. You will be informed of the lengths of cable you require. Imagine that you have finally completed the wall hanging that you have been working on for months, only to discover that it is too large to fit the space available on your wall!

The art of macramé is a wonderful illustration of a craft that dates to the 1970s and the Victorian period. It is an excellent example of how well it is possible to use the current trend of bringing historical items into the home to impart a sense of character into any given space. Macramé in the 21st century, like many other types of fashion, is current and innovative while still paying respect to ancient times. Macramé is a craft that may be used to construct a broad range of products, including wall hangings, plant hangers, pillow covers, and table runners. Macramé is a very flexible craft. It is possible to layer it and arrange it in various ways to ground any space, from a wall covered with plant hangings made of macramé to a couch covered in cushions made of macramé. Craftspeople are creating one-of-a-kind artifacts that have the potential to improve the visual appeal and the perception of depth in any given environment. It is important to enabling a macramé object to stand out, which means that having two or more pieces might reduce the harmony of the area. This is because it is preferable to let the item stand alone. Choose a ceiling hanging or maybe even a cushion made of macramé to mirror the style of the wall sconces and bring the whole thing together. Macramé is a craft that can readily be adapted to suit a variety of design sensibilities because of its adaptability. Boho, contemporary farmhouse, California modern, and Scandinavian are some of the styles that fall under this category.

Chapter 6: Macrame Projects

6.1: Summer Macrame Bag

There are times when all you want is a new purse. Macrame is another craft that you occasionally have some knowledge of. Sometimes you wake up and discover that you can construct your bag using Macrame, and suddenly you're walking around looking like you belong in a magazine! In recent days, there has been a renaissance in Macrame, resulting in a fantastic choice of colorful cotton rope being made available. You might come across this gorgeous mustard color, and a trying to-coordinate set of dark stained wood handles, and you can have the epiphany and use the most fundamental macrame knots to start making a piece of cute equipment that would hold the essentials, such as my wallet, note pad with a pen connected inside the loop binding and phone. The most excellent part is that you can take this texturized handbag with you from summer into fall with its gorgeous golden hue because it is season less.

Tools

- Tape Measure
- Perforated needle
- Cotton Rope
- Scissors
- Tape
- Comb
- Clips

1. Remove thirty-two strands of cotton cord, each about eleven feet in length.
2. Make a lark's head knot with every sixteen strands, then attach it to one of the handles. To tie a lark's head knot, you must first fold each strand in two and then fold the center from the outward rounded section of one end to the

front of the handle. After that, thread the three loose ends through to the center of the folded portion. It results in the formation of a lark's knot.

3. Continue doing so until you have wrapped sixteen strands into each handle. If you don't pay careful attention, all your knots can end on the opposite side of the handle, which would throw off the visual pattern. Utilizing the first four sections of rope on the left side about one handle, begin tying your second row of square knots. You can simplify this process by moving the remaining strands to the side of the screen.

4. To make a "4" form, fold the first strand out over the second and third strands and then fold it under the fourth thread.

5. Then, as illustrated above, fold the fourth line under the 2 and 3 strands, upwards, and over the twist in the first strand. It has the appearance of a heart turned on its side. Pull the two strands on the braid outside when they are snug. This is known as a half-knot.

6. The next step is to build another comparable half knot, but this time you will switch the order in which the outer ropes overlap. The outer rope on the right side will cross over the two ropes in the middle, but it will go under the

extra rope on the left side.

7. The inner rope on that left side will then go behind the two ropes in the middle position and across the curve in the extra rope on the right. Read out stages two to four in this guide on making a macrame stocking for a more in-depth visual overview. This is referred to as a square knot.

8. Create additional square knots by combining the next strands in the chain and continue to add square knots across. The second row of knots we will make will be comprised of alternating square knots.

9. You will need to use the first four strands on the left side. If you want to work only with strands in the middle, skip the first complementary strand on the left side but the last chromatids here on the right side. Make a square knot with these four strands of string using your hands.

10. In your next square knot, use the two previously unused strands on the right side along with the following two strands.

11. Keep going with this starting side of knots. The next step is to complete a row of square knots, followed by a row of switching knots, a row of square knots, and a row of alternating knots.

12. In my pattern, there are just five rows of knots. When working on your second handle, steps were repeated from four through twelve. Put the two handles side by side in this position. My handles both have a top portion and a right side. Thus, it would be most excellent if you were sure that both of your handles are facing the proper way up. Make a square knot with an alternating pattern using two strands with one side of the joint strands from the opposite side of the object.

13. To complete that row, continue tying square knots from the center to each edge, except for the final 2 or 4 strands on either end. After you have completed the tenth row, you can begin leaving some space in between each row. The bottom part of your luggage will allow you more room to move about and stretch out.

14. After completing fifteen rows, fold this bag in halves so that the negative sides of the shoulders face each other and sew the two halves together. Finish out the rows of the bag by simply tying the last knots to attach the beveled edges of the bag.

15. You will see that the knots are tighter together before the top of the chain and further apart at the bottom of the chain.

16. You can make this bag with tassels on the bottom and tuck them within. At this point, flip your bag inside so that the right-hand side of something like the handles faces each other. This is the step you need to take if you want it to be tucked inside like mine.

17. We will tie these knots so that they go from the bottom of the bag on the front side to the bottom of the bag on the other side of the machine.

18. Consider personal strands through one knot on the front half and an isolated string from a near knot on the back side, and then tie a knot in the middle so that they have been as close together as possible.

19. After that, make a double knot. Keep going until all the strands double to a rope on the other side.

20. Make sure that your strands are all the same length by trimming them. If you intend to keep your strands in place on the exterior of your bag, give them a good brushing so that they are complete.

21. Next to that is a yellow macramé handbag, and next to that are gold scissors. Alternatively, you can trim them down even further and then turn your bag inside without the fringe in the end, so trim down further after this shot was taken.

6.2: Macrame Cactus Toy

Among the most gratifying activities is putting effort into beautifying the surfaces of your home, mainly because you may make the very parts that end up hanging on your wall, such as this cactus façade hanging that you see here!

Tools

- Comb
- Masking tape
- Embroidery Needle
- Macrame Cord

- 16-gauge wire

- Embroidery Yarn

1. You will need to begin by cutting two separate strands of macrame cord. You will need one piece of rope cut to 12 inches and another piece cut to 21 inches for a cactus that is 7 inches tall like mine. If you don't secure the end with tape or masking tape, the edges will unravel as soon as you touch them.

2. After that, fold this in half lengthwise and make a mark on both sides around three inches from the bottom. That will end up being on the margins. Now begin by selecting the first color of embroidery yarn you want to use. Wrap it around the macrame rope in a secure manner. Keep your grip on the yarn's end while you conceal it by winding it around to the other side, where you noted the point 3 inches up from the bottom.

3. It is preferable to avoid twisting the six strands of stitching yarn around each other and instead keep them parallel. This will provide you with a higher level of coverage. Be cautious about wrapping everything firmly and not creating any holes in which the macrame rope may be seen passing.

4. Remove some of the embroidery yarn, and then thread a

needle. After that, you should align the two ends, and using the needle, stitch the two cords together by going through each cord. Work your way up through both cords using the hook and yarn in a zigzag motion until you arrive at the top. Make a tight knot, and then cut the yarn to flush.

5. Your inner part is now complete with this.

6. It's now time to begin working on the second portion of the macrame cord that you have. This is the cactus's exterior region, where the arms are located. After marking out three inches from the end, begin wrapping everything with embroidery yarn. I went with a pale shade of green.

7. Once you are getting close to reaching the top, take a length of wire about six inches long, then bend it into the style of a lowercase letter "l," with one inch of each side pointing outward. You will be able to mold the arms and make their point in an upward direction with the help of this wire.

8. You will need to untwist your macrame cord slightly to pull the wire's end in. After that, wrap the embroidery yarn directly over it and the macrame cord.

9. When you reach the top, use a smaller piece of macrame cord or another piece of stitching yarn to create a knot with

a loop. This should only be approximately 1 inch high at most. After that, you will use it as a hanger by weaving it into the head of the cactus.

10. You need to spread the ends on each side, wrap the embroidered yarn over the sides and the macrame cord, and continue working on the other left of the knot.

11. To switch the color of the embroidery yarn, you need to hold the end of both colors to the side that has not yet been finished and wrap the new color around the macrame cords and the two ends of the embroidery yarn.

12. You should attach another wiring arm to the opposite side of the plant. This one ought to be set a notch or two lower. When you are getting close to the surface line, you need to keep checking to see if your wrapping is aligned with the end of the remaining three ends. Therefore, hold the cactus layer that surrounds the layer in the middle so that you can see when to finish wrapping.

13. After you have finished the outermost layer, snip the yarn, so there is a unique advantage and then thread it onto a needle. Now mix the four different layers by going across them all. The Jewelry Manufacturing Flat Nose Pliers are a beneficial tool for pushing and pulling the needles through those layers of dense macrame rope.

14. And finally, remove the blue Kapton tape and tear the edges of it. Using a dog brushing brush or combing fine teeth makes this process much simpler.

15. Using scissors, straighten up the ends as the final stage. It can now be hung or given as a present!

6.3 Macrame Bracelet

Being able to tie a knot in a macrame necklace was essentially a rite of movement for those who spent their childhoods in Southern California near the ocean. Even if those times are a distant memory, we have never lost sight of the incredibly straightforward square knot method. This time, however, we will be swapping out the hemp and wood beads that we used for more contemporary components such as vibrant nylon rope and shiny metal charms. Have fun tying knots!

Tools

- 4 yards of 0.5mm Chinese knotting cord
- Connector or charm or charm
- Lighter (optional)
- Embroidery needle
- Flat nose pliers (optional)
- Pair of scissors
- Clips

1. To begin, cut the cord for knotting into five equal lengths: two of 30 inches, two of 20 inches, and one of 10 inches. After folding the length of the cord that is 20 inches long in half and pulling the loop through into the ring, crinkle the additional half of the cord over the ring and then pull the remaining cord through to the loop. Repeat the previous one to complete this step on the opposite side of the ring. These strands will be anchored, which means they won't move.

2. Locate the midpoint of the upper two strands with the cord that is 30 inches long. Make a fold with the right cord, crossing it over the center strands and tucking it into the

left cord. To complete the process, thread the left cord through the loops on the right side after passing it between the right or middle strands. Pull firmly and bring the knot to the top by sliding it up.

3. Fold the left cord over the middle threads and underneath the right cord to complete the second part of the square knot. To finish, thread the right cord through the loops on the left side after passing it beneath the left & middle strands.

4. Pull extremely hard and continue to repeat the steps left, right, left, right. Continue tying knots until the rope has reached the required length. Remember that perhaps the clasp will add around half an inch to the item's total length.

5. To complete the knots, hook a single cord onto a needle and then sew along the backside, gathering the center of three to four knots at a time. The needle will be easier to draw through to the tight knots using pliers.

6. It is vital to take out the same procedure with the other cord.

7. After you have finished stitching the two knotting cords, clip away any excess. Keep the leftovers, then use a lighter to melt the tips of the scraps to encapsulate them for

additional hold. On the other half of the bracelet, repeat the previous step precisely as it was.

8. Forming the wristband into a circular and overlapping its central strands will create a sliding closure. Make a makeshift knot using the available materials at each end of the cords.

9. Find the exact middle of the strands with the cord 10 inches long. Commence tying square knots in the precise way the bracelet was completed.

10. After reaching approximately half an inch, halt your progress and sew two knotting cords onto the reverse side of a closure. Cut any only transitory links.

11. The two strands in the bracelet's center have been transformed into adjustable ties. Adjust so it fits snugly around the wrist, then tie a knot at each end. Get rid of any unnecessary fat.

6.4: Macrame Coasters

MACRAME COASTER

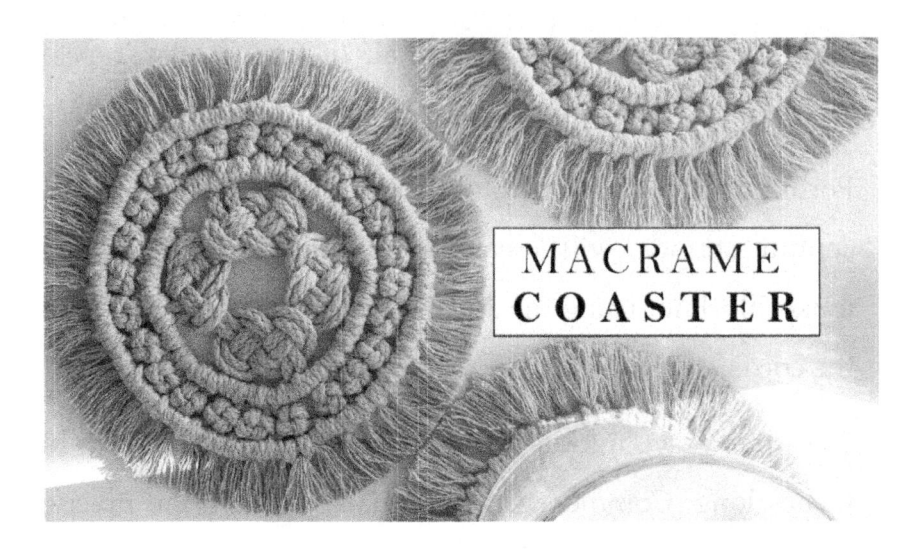

Macrame coasters are the ideal present for birthdays, holidays, or even for oneself. The bohemian aesthetic influences this type of gift. It blows my mind that one can start only with six bits of string and watch it grow into this incredible piece of art that can also be used. You would have never guessed that it could be so helpful.

Tools

- 3 mm macramé cord
- Scissors

1. You'll need to perform a little bit of preparation work before you can get started braiding your coasters together, so get started on that now. To get started, cut the cord you'll be using for macramé into the appropriate lengths.

2. After trimming the lengths of the cords to the desired

lengths, you should put the five smaller cords somewhere else for a couple of minutes and then take the longer cord. Make sure that the end of the string overlaps one aspect of the circle you create with one end of the cord using the string to make a circle.

3. Now take the five remaining pieces of cord and attach them to the main stretch of cord you have been working with.

4. After folding the rope in half lengthwise, position the loop of a cord so that it is underneath the circle. The cord can be wound around the circle by pulling the ends through the loop.

5. Carry on with this technique until all five shorter cords have been fastened to the circle. Pulling the edges of the circle together into a tighter circle will help you construct the center of your macramé coaster.

6. This will also help gather the smaller cords into a cluster. To prevent the strings from becoming untied, tie the main cord's two ends together. A knot called/known as a lark's head knot will be used to complete the last portion of your coaster.

7. The 1st(first) step in tying this knot is to draw the long cord that formed your circle until it is taut and then lay it down

on the table in a horizontal position. This is going to be the cord that all your knots are going to be built on.

8. At last, you will need to pass the end of the shorter string down under the longer string and then through the loops on the left. Doing so will create a tiny loop around your primary string. Tighten the loop and move it closer to the middle of your roller coaster.

9. After that, take hold of the string directly toward your lengthy cord's left. To finish, loop the string's end over the long cord's top after you've pulled it under the cord.

10. You will need to perform the same procedure one more time while using the exact brief string to generate two loops, each of which will use the exact string.

6.5: Macrame Pencil Case

A homemade pencil case is an excellent project for beginning sewers. You can find out how to construct a sewing pattern for a pencil case and add a lining and a zipper by following the steps in this book. To personalize this project and make it uniquely yours, choose an inner fabric that contrasts with the exterior fabric (quilting cotton works beautifully for this), and consider adding fun accessories, such as a fringe or key ring, to the zipper pull.

Tools

- Vanishing Fabric Marker Pen
- Iron
- Pencil
- Zipper Foot
- Outer Fabric
- Lining Fabric
- Sewing Machine
- Scissors

1. Make a rectangle on a piece of paper with the dimensions 23 centimeters by 12.5 centimeters or 5 inches by 9 inches. This piece of paper should be cut out and pinned to the fabric.

2. You will need to cut out four similar rectangles of fabric, two from the lining fabric and two from the outside fabric.

3. Place a lining rectangle so that the correct side faces up, then lay the zip down one edge of the rectangle. Place the outer fabric rectangle, right side down, over the top of the other rectangle. Attach the zip and both layers of fabric by pinning them together. The zip fastener is in the middle of

the two layers of fabric.

4. A sewing machine equipped with a zipper foot was used to sew the zip into place.

5. Sew tight to the teeth of the zipper, going through all layers of fabric and backtracking at both ends using the zipper foot affixed to your sewing machine.

6. Back tacking is when you sew a few stitches, then sew backward over the same stitches, and then sew forwards again. This prevents the stitches from coming loose and leaving holes at the ends of your seams. Back-tacking is also known as backtracking.

7. Unfold the cloth so it is no longer adjacent to the zipper, and then repeat steps three and four on the opposite side.

8. The area around the zipper pull is notoriously tricky to sew in. Stop the needle and thread while the needle is still inserted into the fabric, lift your presser foot, and open or shut the zipper while ensuring the pull is out of the way. This will make the process a little bit simpler.

9. Open the inner fabric aside from the zipper and press each seam, taking care not to contact the plastic teeth of the zipper with the iron because they are located on the zipper.

10. After opening the zipper, pin the two pieces of inner fabric

together with the right wings confronting each other, and then do the same with the two pieces of the outer fabric. Be sure that the zipper ribbon is pinned to face the lining.

11. Make marks on the fabric for the stitch lines using the cloth marking pen. The seam allowance should be 1 cm. Leave a space open at the bottom of a lining fabric; here, we insert our fingers to flip the pencil case so that it is right side out.

12. Sew along the marked lines on the pencil case, beginning on one of the sides of the opening. While maintaining the needle's position in the fabric, pivot the fabric around the corners. Move very slowly as you get to the ends of the zipper; you may need to stop stitching with the needle still in the fabric and lift the presser foot so that you can gently slide the thick material layers through. Back tack should be done on each side of the hole in the lining.

13. Put a pin down on any side of the opening so you remember not to continue sewing past this point.

14. Remove any threads that are hanging loose and cut corners off. Remove any excessive seam allowance from the ends of the zipper. By inserting your hand through the opening and pushing the fabric in the other direction, you may flip the pencil case so that the right side is facing out. To give the corners a good, square point, you can use a knitting

needle or a pencil to poke them.

15. After pulling the lining through the zipper opening, fold its seam allowance so it fits through the gap in the stitching. Do a brief press on this, then stitch it closed, backtracking at either end. Remove any loose threads.

16. Make sure the corners are even as you put the lining back inside, and then use a pencil once more to press out the corners. One last press with the iron and the pencil box is finished!

6.6: Home Décor

Making macrame curtains for your home is a simple project, and the guide can be modified to seem more appealing using yarn in various colors.

1. To begin, knot together four strands on the same foam core board, then insert pins into the top knot and the bottoms of the middle two strands to secure them.

2. Beginning on the right side, take up an outer pink thread, and weave it diagonally across the center two strands to the left. 3. Repeat steps 2 and 1. In the last step of the braid, on the left side of the braid, thread the outer yellow strand under the pink strand, under the middle strands, & over

the pink strand on the other side.

3. Bring the two ends of the rope closer together until a secure connection is made between them. The only matter left to do is do the first step backward. Place the leftmost strand from the outside, now the pink strand, over the two strands in the middle. Apply the same strategy to the use of the other two strands.

4. Using the most recently established successful establishment on the outside as your guide, slide it under the pink strand, then under the two strands in the middle, and then back over the pink to finish the other side. Use your fingers to bring these two threads closer until you reach where they connect the braided strands. This is the most difficult aspect of it! These fundamental steps are repeated throughout everything else that comes after them.

5. Using the second set of four thread strands, repeat steps 1-3 to create a second knot adjacent to the one you just finished making with the first set of strands. Make a new set by connecting the two strands on the right from one knot to the two strands on the left from another knot. This will give you a new set.

6. Please take one of the strands on the right side of the outermost loop and cross it over the two strands in the

middle of the loop facing left, exactly as you did with the first set of strands in step 6. To complete the braid, take the outer left green strand and tuck it under the purple strand, which is located behind the two purple strands in the middle.

7. Bring the two threads closer and pull them as tight as possible. Now go back to the beginning and do everything in the other order! To get this look, wrap the leftmost outermost strand (which should now be the purple thread) over the two strands that are in the middle. To finish the braid, take the strand farthest to the right on the outside (now the green), weave it back and forth under the purple, behind the two strands in the middle, and then to the other side. Bring these two threads together and knot them to ensure they stay put.

8. To split the middle pair of strands, switch the positions of the two strands on the left to the right and switch the positions of the two strands on the right to the left. Make another straightforward knot with both sets and keep continuing like this until you've completed the desired number of rows.

9. To make my time working on the curtain more productive, I divided the rope into 14 pieces, each consisting of four

strands measuring 100 inches. One might create a more aesthetically pleasing knot by using two ropes, each measuring 200 inches in length, and tying them together at the top of the curtain.

10. The knots made in this step are produced in the same manner as the fundamental knots produced in the stages with the yarn, except that they are produced much larger. To complete the design, I tied a knot in the uppermost position of each of the 14 sets. Next, I added a second row of knots below the first set and in the spaces between them (as in the yarn instructions). After that, I moved down one more row and tied knots just beneath the ones I had just created, and I repeated that process with the other rows until I had tied the required quantity of rows. When you finish tying each knot, please take a few steps back to ensure that you arrange them in straight and even rows. When I was tying a sequence of knots around a wooden curtain rod, I ensured they were all the same length by having a ruler nearby and measuring the distance between each knot and the rod. This insured that the knots were all the same size. After completing five rows of knots, I cut the threads and let them hang freely so the curtain could be finished.

11. When you are through braiding the ropes, you have the option of hanging the new curtain in whatever location you choose. After you have clipped the ends, use masking tape (or any comparable white tape; I used "dorm tape") to adhere them down to the floor (the curtain is approximately six feet tall). Remove the tape from the rope so it is still connected to around two-thirds to half of its original length before making another cut. It will assist in preventing the ends from coming undone over time.

6.7: Hammock

Tools

- Stainless steel fittings
- Rope
- Wooden dowels

1. Start by connecting the cotton rope to make a rope hammock.
2. Before anything else, the cotton rope must be secured to one of the hooks on the carbine.
3. After locating the middle of the first length, immediately fold it in half lengthwise to get started. After that, a cow hitch should be used to secure it to the hook. A cow hitch, also

known as the "lark's head" knot or the lanyard hitch, is a macramé knot considered one of the easier knots to tie. The procedure is straightforward. Move the folded end of the rope through the hook in the opposite direction from back to front. Extend your arm and pull the cotton rope's loose ends through the loop to complete the task.

4. Perform this method again, bringing each of the ten rope parts into a secure position.

5. Place the first wooden dowel into the hole.

6. The process of creating the threads for a rope hammock

7. After you have prepared your wooden dowel, incorporate it into the design.

8. Drill ten holes along the dowel's length, ensuring that they are equally separated from one another. Make sure that each item has the same amount of space between them by using a ruler and marking each spot with a pencil. When all the cracks have been drilled, position the steel hook so that it is above the dowel, and then thread each length of rope through the hole that corresponds to it.

9. Weave a macramé pattern onto the cotton rope and make a rope hammock using the cotton rope.

10. Now that you've assembled all the necessary materials, you

may start weaving the cotton rope hammock.

11. Starting on the left, grip the first two ropes and tie an overhand knot to connect them. It is recommended that there be a gap of about two inches between this knot and the wooden dowel. As soon as the first row of knotting is complete, it is necessary to use the technique using the subsequent two ropes, followed by the subsequent two ropes.

12. You should start weaving the second row on the left-hand side again and do so immediately. On the other hand, this time, you should connect ropes two and three together while traveling progressively to the right. Repeating the process while attempting to keep the knots in a straight line may eventually form a sloppy diamond-shaped net.

13. By adding a second dowel, you may increase the support that the rope hammock provides.

14. When the weaving process is finished, and about one meter of rope is left, you may insert the second wooden dowel. Following the same procedure as before, drill ten holes evenly spaced apart down the length of the dowel, and then thread the proper cotton rope through each hole. Check to see that the dowel is positioned accurately.

15. Make sure that the rope's ends are secure.

16. At this point, both ends of the rope must be secured to the second hook on the carbine.

17. Many knots should be used. However, we recommend adopting a double overhand grip. This rather simple procedure will ensure the rope is securely tied and out of harm's way. YouTube also has a multitude of instructional videos that are broken down into step-by-step formats.

18. Suspend the hammock from the branch of a nearby tree.

19. The next step is to secure the rope hammock to the trees that have been chosen.

20. Ensure that the soft-eye splice is pointed correctly before wrapping the excess length of synthetic hemp around the trunk. Apply the same method to the second tree as you did to the first. As soon as you are assured that they are both securely in place, clip each carbine hook into the corresponding soft-eye splice so that the hammock may be joined together. That is the extent of the matter.

6.8: Macramé Leaves and Feathers

Your feeds on social media have recently been flooded with gorgeous feathers made from macrame, yet nobody seemed to be bothered by this. These are being stored away for the possibility that we would one day purchase them and install them in the room where the children sleep. They are a gorgeous group. Then, what exactly is the trick to getting such a silky fringe? After all this time, you finally have the answers at your disposal. In addition to that, it requires the usage of cat brushes. To put it more simply, that is all there is to know about it. Because there are so many variations on this strategy, you may be excited to continue experimenting.

Tools

The following items are required to proceed:

- Fabric shears with a sharp blade
- Cotton string with a single twist every 5 mm
- Fabric stiffener
- Ruler
- Cat brush

The Step-by-Step Guide to Making Macramé Feathers

Using a needle with a 32-millimeter diameter and 1 32-inch thread, cut the required strands again for the spine of medium-sized feathers. Again, ten to twelve threads measuring 14 inches for the top, eight to ten threads measuring 12 inches for the center, and six to eight threads measuring 10 inches for the bottom.

1. Make a fold in the strand that is 32 inches long. One of the strands, 14 inches long, has been folded in half and tucked in below the spine. Another strand measuring 14 inches is divided in half and then put into the loop formed by the upper side strand. Pull it through, then put it down on a nearby strand in a horizontal position. Please ensure that these bottom threads are completely passed through the top loop. You have a knot there in your hair!

2. Keep a strong grip on both sides. The team that is beginning will switch positions in the following row. As a result, something will be placed the second time if you put the vertical thread in place for the first time from left to right. It is necessary to place a second coiled strand inside the loop formed by the first folded thread. After that, pull the upper threads through the lower ones and then pull them further tighter. It is recommended that you continue to get smaller.

3. It is possible to tighten the strands by holding at the bottom of the main (spine) strand, along with one arm, and forcing the strands up. When you are finished, bring the fringes to the bottom of the core thread by dragging them down. After that, would you mind giving it a little snip here and there? This contributes to the smoothing out of

the strands and shaping the shape. The less complicated it is, the fewer strands you will need. In addition to this, it is helpful to have a good pair of fabric shears.

4. After giving the feather a rough trim, place it on a secure surface so that you may have used an ivory brush to brush away the cording. Any surface that is fragile or made of wood will not be surprising. Therefore, I recommend using a piece of cardboard flattened down or a cutting pad that can repair itself. When brushing, begin at the vertebrae and cross the braided rope clockwise. To get that exquisite to create a stunning framing piece, a delicate fringe, you will need to make several firm strokes.

5. Start down. Instead of using the toothbrush to pick out stray strands once you reach the bottom, brush while holding the bottom of a spine in your hand. This will be much more effective. After that, the feather should be made more rigid. Because the line is so thin, any attempt to hang it up will result in it flopping to the ground. We would appreciate it if you could offer a few sprays and at least a few minutes for us to work. You are free to clip your feather after it has completely dried out. To me, this appears to be the difficult part of the process. Treat yourself with kindness. A less amount of pruning is

preferable to a larger one! You may have to adjust the trim depending on when and how the component is relocated. After cutting the fabric, add one more teeny-tiny, small amount of fabric shear as a reference. After that, you'll have the ability to show off your work!

6.9: Wallcoulding Macrame

Macrame was making an excellent comeback this time around in a major way. Macrame has made a significant comeback in recent years. As bohemian décor has emerged as the most popular style, macrame has gradually returned to its hegemony.

The tone, texture, and appearance of macramé are distinctive. Given the growing appeal of hanging artwork in unusual combinations, it is no surprise that macrame designs have enjoyed a renaissance recently. By transforming your pictures, posters, or other beloved images into unique shapes like circles, triangle, hexagons, etc., you may draw attention to any space's organic and creative components. A composite photo frame may be strung in a gorgeously created macrame pattern to create a stunning framing piece. Stringing many macrame strands together with a dowel is an easy technique that everyone can learn. The amazing thing about playing cards is how lightweight they are; you can handle them without even noticing it.

Macrame patterns with Victorian influences are reappearing in craft stores around the country. Furthermore, since there are so many products for sale, this is a good time to look back sometimes and see if anything has changed but if someone else already has purchased it. For those considering launching an Etsy company, there is an excellent step-by-step guide showing how to conduct out all necessary operations, including attaching, cutting, and sewing the macrame patterns. Written macrame instructions are included, along with a thorough list of the materials required and step-by-step instructions.

For those searching for comprehensive macrame instruction, a book may detail all the intricacy and methods required to make the patterns that are presently accessible on the internet. This book has excellent macrame directions. It could occasionally be a little expensive. Consider making a beautiful macrame plant hanger if you're seeking for further incredible DIY macrame crafts to impress your colleagues, family, and neighbors. Besides English and Spanish, it is also accessible in French. Acquiring the knowledge necessary to construct your own planters, book lights, or lovely Victorian lamps. It also offers instructions for creating a beautiful image collage to hang on the wall. From many books, you may discover how to create original DIY macrame patterns. You may create intricate things like the one seen above and below if you possess a basic understanding of how to tie knots. On the other, if you've never learned how and where to tie a knot, it is suggested that you begin with even more fundamental designs. Once you have learned the foundations of knot tying, you will have the skills necessary to create a wide range of lovely, unique items that will improve the appeal of your house and give you a feeling of accomplishment.

How do I Create a Macrame Wall Hanging?

Using these simple guidelines, you may make a macramé door hanging. Study fully. To create a stunning framing piece, understand every facet of Macrame crafts. Begin with a white canvas. You should start at the entry-level and work your way up to the top athlete. Consumers nowadays have a great preference for macrame. Thus, it is presently popular! Modern bohemian or boho ideas often incorporate macrame as a key design element.

Another option would be to continue to inquire, "Is there a method to learn how and where to create macrame? You'll learn all the tricks and enjoy utilizing the Macrame-making method. Any questions you have will be cleared, and all your questions will be addressed. Once you're done, you should have concepts for macrame wall décor that are appealing, reasonably priced, and uncomplicated to construct. You may include the macrame talent on your list of abilities. Macrame may be a great hobby for folks who like crafts and the process of making one-of-a-kind objects from nothing. The finished objects might be traded, given as gifts to family and friends, or kept for one's use.

There are no restrictions on what your mind may conjure up in terms of these problems. You may find anything there, including dream catchers, door decorations, necklaces, bracelets, and other individualized things. As was previously said, people who have never attempted macrame would find it challenging. You can find all the details you need to get started in my guide for beginners to macrame doors. You may make a macrame wall ornament using these simple techniques. You need to make five knots before you can start using Macrame. With your tools, you may also create plant hangers, bangles, and key chains. By mastering these five fundamental knots, you may set yourself on the path to success in macrame.

The rope used in macramé is made of cotton and has the following knots: Double half-Hitch, Lark's Head, Square, Half-Hitch, and Spiral. Macramé wall art also requires a dowel, which may be made of wood or metal, or an analogous limb from a tree or bit of driftwood. Those who hang plants require a hanging ring.

Tools

- Shears,
- duct tape, and
- measurement tape

Creating Wall Hangings

The Lark's Head Strand is the first of them. The Lark's Head knot is perhaps the most significant/basic knot for macrame artists. Once you add wire, this will be the first connection you will learn to tie, and you'll find it in practically every macrame object you come across.

1. Along the cord's length, cut it in two. Replace the loop with your ring, hurdles, or stick. The cord's edges should be inserted into the loop. If you draw the macrame rope tight, you should be capable of tying a Lark's Head knot. For a reversed Lark's Head knot, you may either flip your design towards to the rear or tie it different than usual.

2. The square knot is composed of two primary components. The first side makes a half-square knot, while the second side forms a complete square knot if all sides are finished. Begin by tying two Lark's Tail knots together. You can fit a maximum of four macrame strands in your hand. Cross the peripheral left rope between the two center cords once more to complete the manoeuvre. Attach the outer center cord to the top of the left chord and below the center cables using the outside right cord. Take it now and run through the cycle just on left-hand side of the cloth. Cut the rope with all your strength. This was the original edge of the squared knot, as the name suggests. They are occasionally made available.

3. The simplest kind of fundamental knot is the half hook. Start by tying a Lark's Head tie around your wrist. Take a piece of thread, for instance, and bend it into the shape of

the numeral "4". Thread the rope through hole at the end of the head, and then tighten the knot.

4. Double Full Hitch By tying two half-hitches together at once, it is another triple hitch.

5. A good place to start is with the Lark's Head knot. Create the number "4" using just one rope. The top slot should be used to insert the rope, which should then be tightened. To create another "4" form, repeat the procedure. To make the loop tighter, drag the circuit through it.

6. One of the simplest and most aesthetically appealing helix knots is the spiral knot. You already possess the essential abilities required for success! Simple half-square as well as half-hitch knots may be duplicated to create this knot. Watch careful about the initial half of the round knot shifting to the opposite side after that. Work on the side you previously worked on. You'll see that the Macrame is beginning to create a spiral; do not thwart this process. If you're pressed for time, start by tying two Lark's Face tangles together to create a thick spiral. If you just need a sole or single release, start by attempting to tie a solitary Lark's Head knot, then go on to multiple half hitch knots. It is predicted that there won't be any interference with the twist. Please keep moving ahead. Because it could be

difficult to remain on top of a pattern, pay close attention to this stage.

7. The most crucial thing is to spend time. Yes, put out the required effort. What method is ideal for macrame? What makes a practice so important, specifically? It will stimulate consumer spending as many other abilities do. Therefore, practice is essential before beginning the work.

8. The wooden peg could be used as a training tool. You may practice for an exceptionally long period without becoming fatigued, and it is inexpensive. The idea of a brief practice task is justified by the following. It bridges the time gaps as you wait is for macrame rope to show up. It will help you get familiar with the many types of macrame knots, its names, and the proper techniques for tying them.

9. When your practice macrame project is finished, you'll have the confidence you need to invest the time and materials required to finish your primary or "real" macrame work and reach the water level. Pick the undertaking that you oversee completing. Look for photographs of macrame online.

10. Begin with a little budget! Pay attention to the wall-mounted plant with a cover and the jewelers, including the necklaces and bracelets. Also noteworthy are the

hammocks, table linens, and keychains. The room is decorated with a bed, rug, wreath, or banner, as well as a light source.

11. The most popular starter crafts are now the wall hooks as well as flower holders. You'll have a better idea of how many ropes lengths are required towards the end. Additionally, you could learn more about the project's goals. Find a fashionable appearance that you like. More organic and free form, with jagged corners and instantly recognized patterns.

6.10: Macrame Flower

The addition of macrame flowers is the crowning touch that will make you wall hangings, wedding decorations, and any other macrame crafts seem lovely.

Be advised that to create this macramé flower design, you will need a LOT of rope. Even though it is relatively easy to build (it consists of only two half-hook double knots), however, the flower is rather beautiful.

To make a single flower, you will need around 480 feet with twisted linen macrame ropes with a diameter of 3 millimeters.

Materials required include a macrame board or a corkboard on which to work with T-pins, as well as sixty pieces of braided linen macrame rope approximately three millimeters in diameter with eight feet in length each.

1. In the first step, the outside ropes and the center rope are brought together. You are going to want to take one of the ropes, fold it in half, and then secure it to the wall near your workspace. The remaining 11 segments of rope are going to be tied to the center cord using vertical double half hitches as the knotting technique. Before moving on to the right side, you need to finish tying the vertical double half-hitch knots on the left side. Pull it firmly to make sure the knots are completely new to one another, and then let it go.

2. Move on to Step 2, which entails tying a row of double half-hitches on each side. The next step is to make a row of double half-hook knot all along left edge of a petal. This will complete the petal. At the conclusion of the right side, tie a single final dual half-hook knot to link the two sides.

3. Turn the work around and make a row of double half-hitches pointing the other direction. Once you have located the seventh chords from the left, flip your work so that the left side is staring down, and then tie a row of double half-hook knot in the opposite direction on that chord (to the left). You should tie the knots going to the right, and then repeat the process just on right-hand side, but this time use the rope that is seventh as from right.

4. In Step 4, you will complete a second standard row of double-half hitches by tying them. Repeating the previous step, flip the petal over and make a consistent pattern of double half-hitch knots down both sides.

5. Repeating the previous step, flip the petal over and make a consistent pattern of double half-hitch ties down both sides. After that, turn your item over once again, and starting with the eighth string from the top, create a short row of double half hooked knots facing the opposite way.

6. The sixth step is to complete four rows of double half-hitches in the customary manner. On each side, four rows of double half-hook knot should be done in a regular pattern.

7. Face the work in the other direction as you make the second row of dual half-hitches. Make one additional column of dual half-hitch knots on either side, starting with the ninth thread from the top of the column each time and proceeding in the other direction.

8. At this point, you should have completed three rows of conventional double half-hitches, which is the task for Step 8. On each side, there should be an additional three rows of double half-hook knots knotted in a consistent fashion.

9. At this point, you should finish the final row. To finish off

[118]

the project, tie one double half-hitch knot according to usual procedure. After that, take the working cable from the knot, and then use the filler cord to secure it. The following dual half-hitch knot should be tied around both ropes. That step must be repeated for each knot. Make careful to do all surfaces.

10. At this point, you should attach the flowers. To form the flower, first raise two of the strands on every flower, as seen in the photo below, and then gather all the flowers together. Overlapping the petals is one way to make a flower seem more realistic.

6.11: Macrame Boho Tassel

The process goes quickly and simply. For this project, you'll need a length of rope, a kitchen knife, and an open afternoon.

Tools

- 15-20 lengths of 3- or 5-mm twisted silk rope, each measuring 12 inches.

- For the hanging portion, a single 15-inch piece of 3-ply thick rope will be utilized.

- 10 feet of 1mm twisted rope were cut for the macrame components.

- Blades Coarse comb

Making a Tassel

1. Gather around 15–20 strands of rope and softly fluff them in the middle to start. Then, securely knot them together in the middle using the rope with such a 1 mm diameter.

2. the rope that initially linked them all should now be laying on its side. Next, grab hold of the knots and turn them around. To make the fibers look consistent, brush them once again, splitting them into the left and right sides.

3. The next step is to take the yarn with larger diameter, fasten the ends, and then thread the tassel through it. Join the two rope ends back together so that the hanging section's knotted ends are hidden in the center of the tassel and the remaining rope is loose but still in place. Give this another brush if required.

4. At this stage, the tassel must be knotted. You may tie a gathering tie, as shown in the illustration below, or a standard overhand tie. In any event, make sure the knot is just as solid as possible! All that is needed when the tassel is complete is a fast brushing and trimming.

5. Take a thin rope with a diameter of 1 mm and cut this into 12 to 14 parts. Make sure that each piece is around three times as big as the tassel they are producing. The parts may be held together either by hanging them on them or by putting a lark's tail knot around them. In the beginning, make sure they completely round your tassel, but then tie them on firmly. Make sure there are an equal number of objects by counting them.

6. We'll use the square tie, a basic macrame knot, to give your tassel a little more flair without changing how simple it is.

7. The square knot consists of two parts that are mirror reflections of one another and requires four threads or ropes (thus the exact number we have previously mentioned). You may choose to start reading from the left or on right side of a page. We are initially moving to the right!

8. Beginning just on right side, attach the rope perpendicularly to the other three parts using the rope that

is farthest to the right. Next, move the component that is furthest to the left below it, after that behind the one in the middle, and then through the loop. It is advised that you examine the images since they more clearly depict the knot.

9. Bring your partially knots to a top and then repeat the procedure, starting with the other side. You will see that the knot is made up of three lines after you are done tying it: two horizontal and just one vertical. Tie a full row of knots all the way around the tassel to complete it.

10. You may either tie one or 2 more lines of square knots to finish your tassel, or you can shape it into a triangular by placing three knots in the initial row, two in the second row, and one in the middle of the third row.

6.12: Macrame Garlands

The best aspect of this project is how much color and intrigue it adds without taking up a ton of work or materials, making it the perfect project for decoration ideas at gatherings or even for a wedding due to how little work and materials are needed.

Tools

- Scissors
- Yarn in a variety of colors,
- Pushpins, or
- Washi tape.

You are free to cut the yarn whichever long you like for your foundation. It can be cut down to around an 8-foot length. After that, depending on the amount of fringe look you want, cut it yarn in pieces that are about two to three feet long. However, the length of them will decrease the more you tie them together. You may easily cut them into smaller pieces to create them later. To produce a garland this big, you may only need around 30-35 individual pieces of yarn.

1. Push pins should first be used to fasten the base strand to the wall. Next, add the various components by dangling a single knot so over base.

2. After that, start tying double knots the with fourth and third strands of yarn to start the rear row of knots by omitting the first strand of yarn. The knots on the rear row will start here. Place in the middle, about two inches below the base.

3. Following, tie the next two layers of thread together about two inches down, ensuring sure they were mostly centered between the knot on the foundation piece of yarn. Once the

job is finished, keep doing this.

4. A next is to tie a knot with the first and third strands at the start of the row number to start the rear row of knots. The next phase is adding more knots across, starting about 2 inches underneath the most recent one. You should once again go to the left edge after you have completed the second row. After knotting both second and third strands once more, let the first strand alone and repeat the process until you reach the opposite side.

5. You may stop here or make more knot rows, but you can also choose to keep a little piece of fringe dangling off the end. Trimming your ends to the same length will be your last step before you're done.

Chapter 7: How To Avoid Principal Error?

Making Macrame is more than a relaxing pastime for creative types. You can use it to make ornamental or artistic furniture pieces for your house or workplace, as well as presents or even products to sell. Keep reading to find out where to Macrame with the help of this simple guide. Keep reading to learn the basics of easy Macrame for starters and get started making one-of-a-kind works of art. Macrame is a form of handicraft that has been around for millennia but has recently seen a wave in popularity. It's plausible since it uses readily available, low-priced, and ubiquitous materials. Learning to do Macrame is a skill that can be used well after learning how and when to Macrame, you will be able to produce bohemian home decor, including a macrame wall sconce or flower hanger and accessories as tasseled purses. The great news is that it is not exceedingly difficult, particularly with our step-by-step photo guides to the seven critical knots used in Macrame. Macrame is a textile craft that involves creating patterns by tying beautiful knots with string or macrame cord.

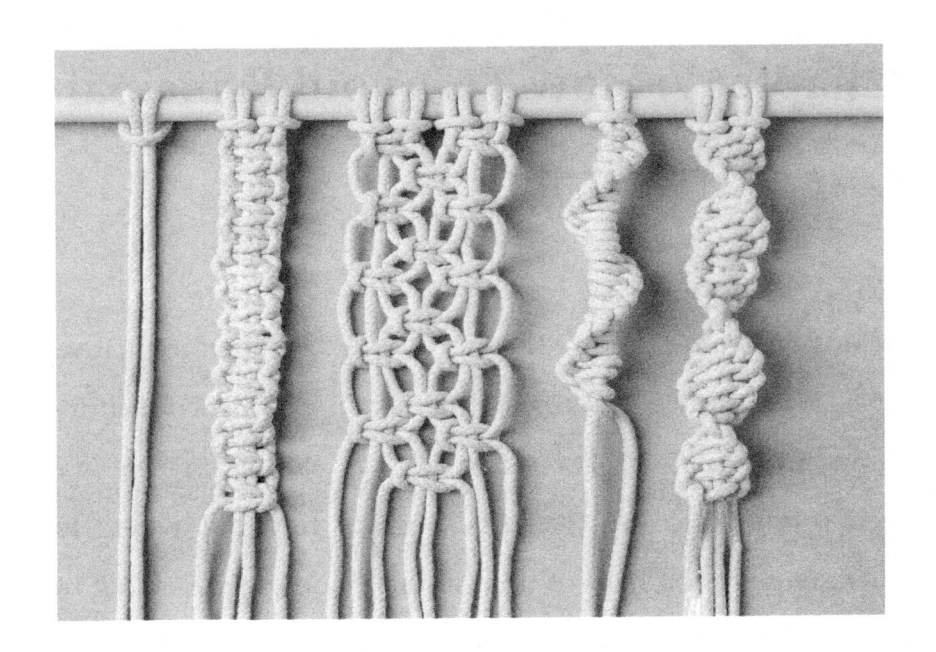

These designs can manufacture various items, including traditional plant hangers, bags, jewelry, and wall hangings. It is thought that Arab weavers were the first to use Macrame. The technique subsequently made its way to Italy and Spain before making its way to the United Kingdom in the seventeenth century. In the 1970s, Macrame was at the peak of its fame, and everything from macrame planters and dream catchers to macrame owls was made using the technique. Over the previous decade, we have witnessed a growing enthusiasm for handcrafted goods, natural materials, and crafts in general. Macrame has also made a comeback, and its sleek and natural patterns can be found just on the high street in addition to on fashion runways and luxury furnishings. The Bohemian vibe is in style now, and Macrame has also returned.

Put that rough cotton from the 1970s behind you. Nowadays, everything must have a string, leather, or cord made of soft cotton. To create an item using the macrame technique, one must tie a rope or cord using at minimum one macrame knot. Knitting and weaving are two examples of additional craft methods you could use. Many of you have probably seen photos of beautiful macrame decorations, like wall hangings and plant hangers, on Snapchat or media websites. It's conceivable that you don't know what "macrame" means. Macrame is an art and craft that involves tying knots in a colorful pattern to make different kinds of patterned textiles. Most of the time, it is done by hand instead of using needles or other tools. Because of this, Macrame has become a popular way to make things for citizens who like to do with their hands. Macrame is a craft that can be used to get a wide range of arts, but instead, decorations, such as jewelry, bracelets, wall hangings, throw pillows, and more. This is because Macrame is flexible and can be used in many ways. Most people don't mean to make mistakes. They also can't be stopped. You will always make a mistake at some point. Mistakes happen, and a decent leader knows that. It occurs if the same mistakes keep happening or when mistakes happen a lot. No matter how understanding a leader is, mistakes can't be ignored, and work can't be done without care. Even if you cringe when you think about your mistakes, they don't make you a bad worker. If anything, they are great ways to learn how to do things better. For my career, I've made my fair share of mistakes.

7.1: Study Basic Knot

Macrame is an art form that employs numerous types of knots. Some are less involved and more direct than others. In addition, a handful of fundamental knots need to be mastered by newcomers to the macrame knotting method. Let's say you want to start a macrame craft. It would be best if you learned these basic knots and used them as building blocks to make your unique knot combinations. The four classes into which these knots can be sorted are the Mounting, the Square, the Hitch Tangle, and the Gather Knot. As the name implies, mounting knots are superficial knots used to fasten cords to a mounting point, such as a hardwood band or metal hoop. The two most frequent knots for Mounting are the lark's head knot and the inverse lark's head knot. A square knot, half-square knot, or spiral knot (sometimes called a square knot or half-square knot) is one of the most often used knots in macramé. A square knot is tied with four ropes: two outside cords (also known as working cords) and two inside cords. With so many possible variations, the adaptability of this class of knots is through the sky. Hitch knots & their variants are more complex to tie than the ones we've covered so far, making them challenging for beginners to learn.

On the other hand, hitch knots can be used to make a variety of attractive designs. The half-hitch knot and the double half-hitch knot are the two most common types of hitch knots. Gathering knots are a collection of knots used to finish a task like a macrame planter, as the term suggests. Regarding their practicality, the overhand & wrapping knots are two common gathering knots. To prevent a rope or two cords from unraveling, the former is typically employed at the end of the project, while the latter is used either at the beginning or the end of the endeavor to secure a collection of strings.

7.2: Start With Hemp Cord

First, divide the braided rope into 20 and 70 inches. Make sure you fold both pieces in half. Make a loop by making a knot in both cords at the midpoint. The loop must be large enough to fit the bead that will serve as the clasp. We severed the hemp rope into manageable lengths. There will be four slack lines. The primary supporting chords (the shorter cords) should be positioned in the center, and the four tying cords (the longer cords) should be positioned outside.

Cross the left tying cord over the anchor lines. You can complete the knot by crossing the right tying cord over the left one. To do this, pass the right linking cord through the loop shaped by the left tying cord and then slide it under the cords that serve as anchors. Holding both ends of the rope firmly, raise the knot until it rests on the object. If you want to repeat steps 3-6, ensure you start with the right tying cord the second time. Alternate between the left-tied cord and the center-tied cord indefinitely. Beads are added by stringing them onto the central strands of support cords and then pushing them up to the topmost knot. Start the next knot under the bead using the same tying cord. Make sure the bead is in place by snugly drawing both tying ropes. When you've reached the desired length for your bracelet, add more beads, and continue tying knots in alternate patterns.

Wrap the last bead, a clasp bead, around the ends of all four strands. Gather all the strings and tie them into a knot as close to the clasp bead as possible. Cut the extra cord and throw it away. With your newfound knowledge of square knots, you should be able to construct a macramé bracelet. Congratulations! To find out how many beads you'll need to make your bracelet the width you want, design a pattern for the beads. If you've already tied several cords together and can't remember which one to use for the next knot, look for a protrusion in the cable to determine where you last left off. The next knot must

be tied, beginning with the side that has the hump.

7.3: Use Right Materials and Equipment

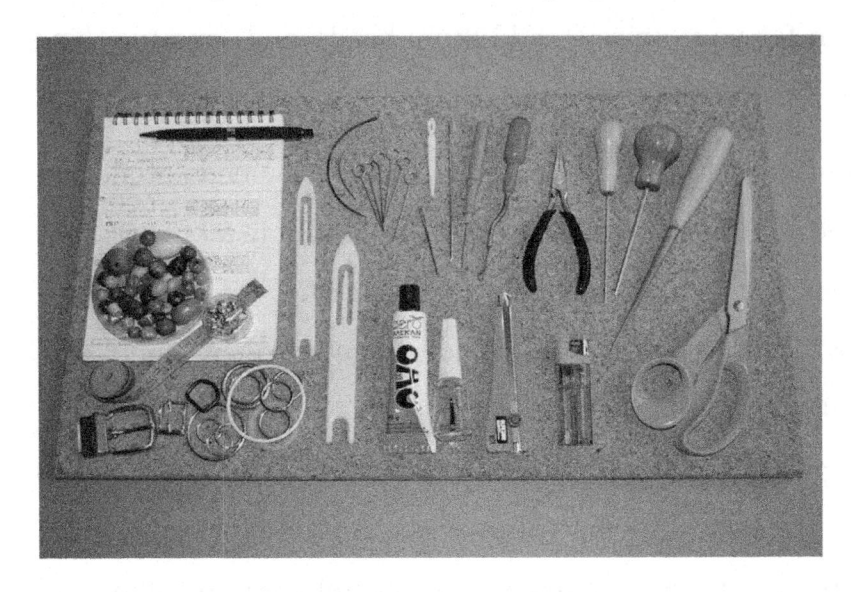

Macrame can be done with various cords, including cotton, acrylic, nylon, and string cords, with a twist that resembles a rope. These cords can be found at craft and home improvement stores. Working with a cotton rope that is at least 3 millimeters in diameter is my personal preference. There are two distinct varieties of cotton rope. A cotton rope that has been braided and twisted. Cotton strands are combined into a single rope to create braided cotton rope with as many as six strands. 3-strand rope, also referred to as 3-ply rope, in which the individual strands are twisted around one another. Although standard rope typically has three strands, I've seen it made with four strands before. I adore it since it is simple to work with, exceptionally tough and long-lasting, and can be unraveled at ends to form a fabulous fringe.

Warehouse organization is greatly aided by using efficient material handling equipment, which leads to fewer lost products and supplies. It will consequently take less time to get merchandise from your warehouse. You'll be more productive because of the money and time savings. Keeping your warehouse neat depends on effectively managing the materials stored inside. Because of this, customers will have a much simpler time locating the products they need, and the amount of time mandatory to complete their orders will decrease. This helps you save cash and please your customers by getting their orders to them quickly. Product damage due to inefficient handling and warehousing can significantly raise manufacturing costs. Evidence suggests that taking care while handling materials and components might help keep costs down. Investing in suitable storage for the company warehouse allows you to make the most of existing space and reduces the risk of crashes affected by people tripping or falling.

7.4: Start With a Simple Project

Macrame is an art form that encourages creativity via the use of knots. If you've never tied a knot, I recommend starting with a square one. Either the Square or alternated square knot can be used to tie this. Both approaches are discussed in detail below. Most modern macramé relies on this tie, which is ideal for amateurs because of its ease of use. As a versatile craft, Macrame can be used for many purposes. Once you've mastered the various knotting techniques, you'll be ready to design your unique designs and give life to your handmade macramé creations. Some well-known macrame projects for decorating with scales, small and large, are listed below. Here are some thoughts: You can use macramé to construct various practical and decorative items, such as a keychain, bracelet, plant hanger, bag, pillow cover, or table runner to add color and pattern to your everyday life—macrame blanket to wrap yourself in at night. Your gorgeous windows could benefit from a Macrame swing, Macrame canopy, Macrame wall hanging, Beadwork hammock, or Macrame swing Macrame curtain.

7.5: Keep The Ends from Fraying

Place a piece of tape around the cording at the location where you intend to cut it. Cut the cord to flush with the tape strip to guarantee that both ends are encased in tape. The end of the coding that has been taped should have enough white art paste or seam coolant treatment applied to it. Before getting rid of the tape, be sure the sealant or adhesive has had enough time to dry. It shouldn't get more than a few minutes for the sealer or adhesive to dry. If, while removing the tape, you observe that the twine is unraveling, you should apply additional sealant or glue. Before continuing to work on the project, ensure that the coat has had sufficient time to dry. Wrapping both ends of the cable is a good idea if you purchase it from a fabric store. Similar applications of sealant or glue should be used to adhere to both ends of the cording. In addition, seal any fresh cuts you make while cutting a piece of dowel rod from an individual collection. Cord whipping is one of the more conventional procedures that can be used to avoid fraying the cord. The rope ends are secured by a flax string that is wrapped tightly around them using this way. This procedure will result in a clean and professional finish and stop the rope from fraying. Splicing is an efficient method that can be used to terminate the rope without necessarily having to use a knot. Using this technique, the cord was looped back on itself and then interlaced to make a firm or soft eyelet. In comparison to the use of whipping, this technique has proven to be the most long-lasting one. This is an excellent choice for use in demanding situations. You will need to use a hot seal to create a smooth and firm plastic to tie the fibers together and stop them from fraying. Products made from natural fibers are a good fit for this method. You can also utilize a hot knife and seal the ends, which will prevent them from being frayed in the future. To accomplish this, you will need to place a cord on a substantial piece of thermally tile or concrete and then gently press the blades against the fibers of the cord.

However, because natural fibers are susceptible to damage from heat, this technique is only suitable for synthetic fibers. This method is the least complicated. However, it can only be used on synthetic fibers. When heating the cord, it is a great option to do so with a blowtorch because this will ensure that the fibers are heated uniformly and will result in a clean fusion at the cord's end. Back-splicing is a straightforward process that yields excellent results. In addition, it does not impact the strength properties of the rope in any way, and it does not involve the purpose of any materials, excluding the rope itself. Untwist a portion of the end of the rope you have twisted. It depends on the rope portion one wants re-incorporated into the rope itself.

To create a reliable back splice, you only need a few tucks to secure the ends of the yarn. Make a knot in the form of a crown. Make sure that each of the three strands is facing away from the remainder of the rope once you have separated them. Please take one of the strands and wrap it around in a counterclockwise direction over the one next. You should now take the string you have already crossed over the first rope and place it over the other two strands in a counterclockwise direction. The end of the last strand will be threaded through the loop formed by the first strand. Pull the rope through the knot to tighten it; this should result in a triangle forming at the ends of the rope. Take one end and cross it over the strand that is closest to it, then go under the strand that is closest to that strand. Please take the next strand, cross over the one closest to that end, then travel beneath the strand immediately adjacent to it. Take the last strand, cross it over the one closest to the end, and then go beneath the one closest to the end. Repeat this process step as often as necessary until the ends are entirely re-braided into the rope.

7.6: Make Uniform Knotting

Once you've mastered the basics of macramé, you may start paying more attention to details like even spacing between knots. Consistency in tension and a straight line of knots in all three aspects are essential. Try to find edges and loops that are equally substantial as you go. For the quickest and most reliable results, it is recommended to use a macrame board or another anchoring device to keep your work in place as you go. The Macrame panel will assist you in keeping the pattern of your project and the strength of your knots uniform. The most significant way to learn to tie knots consistently is to practice, which will help you master the skill. Keep any scraps of cordage for future use in learning new knots. As you gain experience, your knots will resemble those of a professional. That's the secret to creating a beautiful macrame. After you've tied the first knot, make it a habit to double-check your work. You won't have to waste time or energy on it. Loops in your macramé projects will eventually line up and be the same size as you gain experience. The result is a more uniform appearance. Because of this, the Macrame will look fantastic!

7.7: Be Patient

Lastly, being patient is the key to cracking Macrame and be the head of knotting. Although the science of perseverance is still in its infancy, mounting evidence suggests that practicing it may benefit our physical well-being. Schnittker and Emmons discovered in their research conducted in 2007 that persons who were patients were less likely to describe health problems such as headaches, acne flare-ups, ulcers, diarrhea, and pneumonia. The path to success is challenging, and impatient people who want to see their efforts pay off right away may be willing to follow it. Consider the recent criticisms millennials have received for their unwillingness to "pay their dues" an unskilled laborer and for moving quickly from one position to another without growing and learning in their careers. When one is connected to other people, patience transforms into a sort of kindness. Please think of the best friend who stays up with you night after night to console you through the heartache that won't go away or the granddaughter who beams with happiness despite having heard her grandfather tell the same story dozens of times. These are examples of people who are there for you when you take them the most. According to the findings of specific studies, people who practice patience are more likely to be cooperative, compassionate, equitable, and forgiving. In

Schnittker's study in 2012, she invited 71 undergraduate students to participate in two days straight of patience training. During this time, the participants learned how to recognize feelings and the triggers that accompany them, regulate their emotions, empathize with others, and meditate. Within two weeks, participants indicated experiencing higher amounts of pleasant emotions, feeling less depressed, and having more patience with the problematic individuals in their lives. To put it another way, it seems like patience is a talent you can exercise below — and practicing it could benefit overall mental health.

Conclusion

People have been thinking about what art is since the beginning of written history. Tolstoy thought that the purpose of art was to help us understand each other, while Anas Nin thought it was a way to get rid of our excess emotions. But the highest level of artistic performance might be something that bridges the gap between the two: a way to bring empathy into our minds so that we can both get rid of and better understand our feelings. In other words, it would be a type of therapy. Macramé has changed over time. Yes, it's all part of the creative process, which goes on differently at different times. Both people who are new to macramé and people who have been doing it for a long time enjoy how relaxing, fun, and creative it is. People who want to use and enjoy the things they make with macramé are finding increased ways to make beautiful items that match their home's style, clothes, and sense of style.

Macramé is a craft that has become increasingly popular because it looks nice, is easy to decorate, and makes our homes feel more like us. Macramé is a methodology that can be employed for many different projects and gives you many ways to be creative. With macramé, you can make things like wall hangings, hangers for flowers, clothes and accessories, and textiles for the home. It can be utilized to start from nothing and build something, or it has the potential to decorate something made differently. Some projects made with macramé are jeweler, plant hangers, home decor, wall hangers, purses, belts, and everything else. Macramé comes in many colors and textures, granting you a lot of choices. Different thicknesses of natural fibers and hemp are used, as well as twine, dyed nylon, polyester fibers, and even a mix of the two. Beads made of glass and clay are being used through projects along with wooden beads, and this is a tendency that is likely to continue. When used with other tools, art can give us abilities beyond what science has given us. When we are born with certain flaws in our minds instead of our bodies, we can use art to make up for these mental frailties.

Made in the USA
Las Vegas, NV
07 November 2023